AF338229

To Maria Palmeiro

OTAVIO
LEONIDIO

RISKY
SPACE

LATIN AMERICA: THOUGHTS

Romano Guerra Editora
Nhamerica Plataform

MANAGEMENT COORDINATION
Abilio Guerra, Fernando Luiz Lara and Silvana Romano Santos

RISKY SPACE
Otavio Leonidio
Brasil 3

EDITOR
Abilio Guerra, Fernando Luiz Lara and Silvana Romano Santos

EDITORIAL STAFF
Silvana Romano Santos, Fernando Luiz Lara, Abilio Guerra
and Fernanda Critelli

GRAPHIC DESIGN
Maria Claudia Levy and Ana Luiza David (Goma Oficina)

FORMATTING
Fernanda Critelli

EBOOK FORMATTING
Natalli Tami

TECNICAL REVIEW
Nathalia Perico

TRANSLATION
Carlos Eduardo Dias Comas, Fernando Luiz Lara,
Gabriel Pomerancblum, Giovana Sanchez, Luca Senise,
Nick Rands and Otavio Leonidio

TRANSLATION REVIEW
Fernanda Critelli, Fernando Luiz Lara and Otavio Leonidio

Romano Guerra Editora

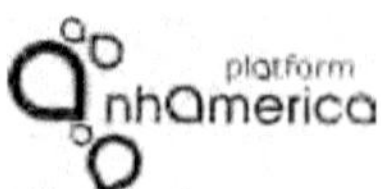

SÃO PAULO

AUSTIN

2017

OTAVIO
LEONIDIO

RISKY
SPACE

FOREWORD

I wrote the texts in this compilation over ten years. With the exception of "Angelo Bucci, Risky Space," all were written at my own risk. That is, they are the product of a very personal intention – namely to publicly address subjects and issues that captured my attention at different points in time. Looking back, I can clearly tell what those subjects and issues were.

The first subject is Lúcio Costa. Both of the texts that focus on his ouevre ("Lúcio Costa, Critique and Crisis" and "In Search for the Words of Our Master") are developments of my doctoral dissertation, which I defended in 2005 at Pontifícia Universidade Católica do Rio de Janeiro. Whenever I addressed Costa's writings, it was in order to understand how he managed to account for the questions that challenged the leaders of Brazilian modernist movement. And what became clear to me is that, without Costa's utterences, Brazilian modern architecture as we know it would never have existed.

The second subject is Brazilian modern architecture itself – more specifically, the power of its presence in the contemporary scenario. "Christian de Portzamparc, the Invader," "Álvaro Siza Vieira, Another Void" and "Angelo Bucci, Risky Space" are all essays that take the architecture of Oscar Niemeyer, Affonso Reidy and the like as a bench mark for works as diverse as those of Portzamparc, Siza and Bucci. But the texts also the wish to problematize the notion of heritage itself – in this case, a heritage that always seemed to me more embarrassing than beneficial. Hence my interest in the work of Lelé – which, not by chance, constitutes the most relevant isolated fact in Brazil's contemporary output.

The third subject are the nexuses between contemporary art and architecture – phenomena that I address here either in tandem ("Concretism, Neo-concretism and the Contemporary," "Guy Debord and Robert Smithson" and "The Foster-Eisenman Complex") or in standalone form ("Hal Foster, History and the Real"). The main difference from the first two subjects is that in the latter case, Brazil ceases to be the locus of enunciation. This choice reflects both a personal motivation (ridding myself of an atavistic localism) and the perception that, in order to address the contemporary, I had to muffle the typically Brazilian voice that pervades the previous texts.

Text selection took shape in conversations with Abilio Guerra and Fernando Lara, with input from Silvana Romano. Without their dedication this book would not exist.

ANGELO BUCCI
RISKY SPACE

TRANSLATED BY GABRIEL POMERANCBLUM

NOT LONG AGO, I WROTE THAT ONE OF THE MOST REMARKABLE ASPECTS OF ANGELO BUCCI'S WORK IS THE COMPLEX RELATIONSHIP IT ESTABLISHES BETWEEN STRUCTURE AND SPATIALITY. I WAS REFERRING, ON THAT OCCASION, TO ONE SPECIFIC PROJECT, NAMELY THE CARAPICUÍBA HOUSE, DESIGNED BY BUCCI AND ALVARO PUNTONI — IN MY VIEW, ONE OF THE BEST PROJECTS OF THE LAST FEW YEARS IN BRAZIL.[1]

An analysis of Bucci's recent work suggests that the design of that small house somehow sums up the inner principles of his architecture.

I reiterate my argument: As many Brazilian architects, that is to say, as direct descendants of Oscar Niemeyer and Affonso Eduardo Reidy, Bucci and Puntoni paid very close attention in this house to the design of the structure. The operation is not restricted, however, to reproducing some of the structural recurrences in Brazilian modern architecture.

Granted, some of these recurrences are present in the project at hand – namely: a) the typically Niemeyer-esque exiguousness of columns and pillars (in this case, two large columns that support the volume of the office atop the set); and b) the rhythmically sequenced structural porticoes which support roof and floor slabs, much like what Reidy does at the Museum of Modern Art in Rio de Janeiro – MAM (in Carapicuíba, two parallel, rectangular porticoes that support the building's floor slabs).

The essence of the operation, however, is not limited to that. What sets the project apart is the way it explores the plastic and spatial effects of the unusual juxtaposition of these two structural gestures, which are treated here – and this is the key point – as two autonomous entities.

To say that the project's spatiality coincides with or stems from the design of the structure is insufficient, therefore. Rather, it is the complex, hybrid resultant of the juxtaposition of structural entities which are not only endowed with specific morphologies, but which also generate spatialities of their own. The project's formal and, above all, spatial quality, therefore,

RESIDES LESS IN THE JUXTAPOSITION OF ITS BUILT ELEMENTS THAN IN THE COLLISION OF THE EMPTY SPACES (OF THE VOIDS!) THAT EACH OF THESE STRUCTURAL ENTITIES INDEPENDENTLY PRODUCE.

The Carapicuíba project is one of the most complex and sophisticated developments of a research that began some two decades ago. The terms of the investigation seem clear enough to me: As I said, Bucci set out to explore the potentialities of the structure-spatiality relationship. The theme is not altogether new. Since the 1930s, Oscar Niemeyer and Affonso Eduardo Reidy relied on it to constitute their seminal oeuvres, which throughout the second half of the 20th century, shaped the architecture of so-called São Paulo

School – the architecture of Vilanova Artigas, Lina Bo Bardi, and Paulo Mendes da Rocha, among others. Bucci's work, evidently, belongs to that lineage. Each new project is for him an opportunity to rearticulate a reasonably limited structural

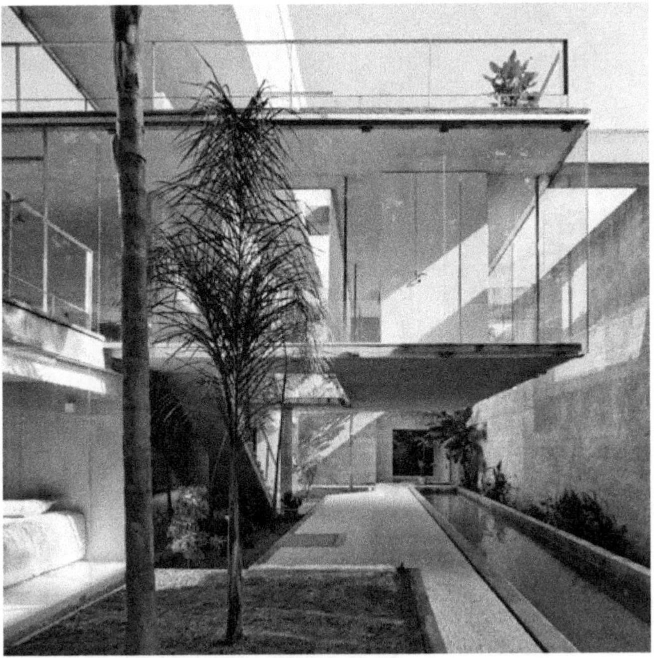

House in Carapicuíba, Carapicuíba SP. Angelo Bucci and Alvaro Puntoni, 2003-2008. Photo Nelson Kon

and formal repertoire. Which explains why his designs appear to be variations of one and the same theme.

Not all developments are as complex as the house in Carapicuíba. As a matter of fact, some of them are exceedingly simple – which does not mean less interesting. A good example is the house in East Hampton, designed in 2007. Here, there isn't any hybridism in the structure's design, composed of two lengthy inverted beams, running parallel and very close to one another, which support the flat roof slab. The arrangement of the items that comprise the building's program is also reasonably simple, with living areas divided into two independent sectors: living room and kitchen are in the

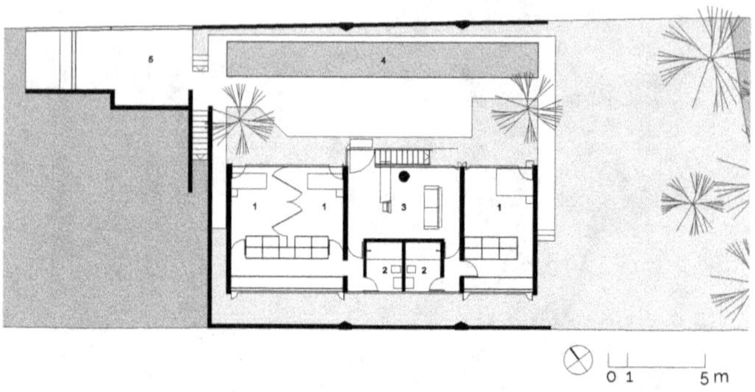

House in Carapicuíba, living floor, Carapicuíba SP. Angelo Bucci and Alvaro Puntoni, 2003-2008. SPBR Arquitetos Collection

top floor, while the bedrooms, the garage, family room, and remaining elements are in the half-buried ground floor.

At once, the project evokes two icons of 1950s Brazilian modern architecture – namely, Lina Bo Bardi's Art Museum of São Paulo – Masp, and Oscar Niemeyer's Casa das Canoas [Canoas House]. From the former, Bucci's building inherits a rather unorthodox way of employing the principle of the repeating structural porticoes. Indeed, just like in Bo Bardi's building (and in contrast to what happens in Reidy's MAM), the sequence of porticoes does not run in the same direction as the building's spatial expansion, or better yet expansibility. This entails a sort of semantic uncertainty: Are these elements really porticoes or instead pillars and beams?[2]

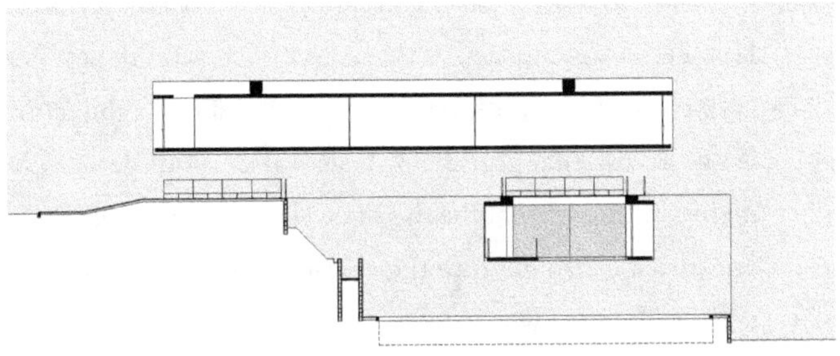

House in Carapicuíba, longitudinal section, Carapicuíba SP. Angelo Bucci e Alvaro Puntoni, 2003-2008. SPBR Arquitetos Collection

From Niemeyer's residence, in turn, the East Hampton house borrows the classical compositional principle of the mineral pedestal (half-buried in both cases; fragmented in Bucci, and partly hidden in Niemeyer) topped not by a solid object, but instead by a habitable void (defined by a horizontal concrete slab). While sections suggest a connection with Niemeyer's house, as well as the reliance on the classical model, floor plans render explicit an inversion in the terms of the composition: Whereas, in Niemeyer, plastic freedom is ascribed to the flat roof slab, and formal restraint to the pedestal, in Bucci the opposite holds true. This compositional *parti* (and I believe that here, unlike Carapicuíba, it really makes sense to speak of *parti* and composition) commands other projects of Bucci's, notably the PUC-Rio media library.

The affinity with the architecture of Niemeyer, Reidy and Lina Bo Bardi emphasizes the aspect of continuity between Bucci's work and the tradition of modern Brazilian architecture. This is not an original argument. It was after all under suspicion of mere continuism that the then-newly graduated Bucci found himself thrust overnight into the epicenter of Brazilian architectural debate. The year was 1991, and project selection was pending for the Brazilian pavilion at the Seville Exhibition due the following year. A public competition was held; 253 teams entered, many comprising renowned Brazilian architects. To the surprise of many, the contest was won by a team of three young men fresh out of school: Alvaro Puntoni, José Oswaldo Vilela, and Angelo Bucci.

The result wreaked havoc. In a controversial, now-famous article, suggestively entitled "Deu em vão" (a play on words with "em vão," which means both "in vain" and "free span," which is a trademark of the architecture of São Paulo School), critic and historian Hugo Segawa harshly censured the contest's jury – which included Paulo Mendes da Rocha – for picking "a known, predictable, and therefore conservative architectural line."[3] Even today, some point to the outcome of the competition as the cornerstone of the "modernist revival" that presumably has reigned in Brazil since then.

To read Bucci's work from the perspective of continuity is, however, misleading. For by all accounts, Brazilian architecture as a whole, and São Paulo architecture in particular, are for Bucci essential references – but not sacred totems. His later output shows how little interested he is in simply reproducing the formal and structural findings of Brazil's modernist tradition.

Once again, let us focus on the design of the structure, notably to the trend toward a reduced numbers of pillars and the extensive use of stayed slabs.[4] There are many plausible explanations for these recurrences. Personally, I don't think that it merely reflects the Corbusian principle of socializing the ground floor of buildings (hence his proverbial eulogy of pilotis). Instead, I think it expresses the somewhat obsessive drive of Brazilian modern architects (devoted as they were to the project of modernizing a rural, underdeveloped country) to demonstrate the national ability to overcome the myriad of constraints which, in architecture as much as in other domains of culture, were bound to prevent Brazil from attaining modernity. The obsession with the formalization of the structural work should be read, in this sense, as a typical case of symbolic form – a metonymy of the heroic cultural effort employed in Brazil's forceps-based modernization project. Hence, in the specific domain of architecture, of the recurrent and – in my view, embarrassing – aspect of structural prowess and virility which characterizes some of the most iconic modern Brazilian buildings. As if erecting a building with a limited number of columns and few slender steel cables equated to erecting Brazilian society as a whole.

Now, if the need to affirm potency and virility could once fit the bill of Brazil's conservatist modernization process, obviously that is no longer the case today. Times have changed. To simply reenact it in our times would lead to pure anachronism, as attested by Oscar Niemeyer's recent work.

Bucci's use of the national tradition of exiguous points of support and stayed slabs demonstrates how far removed the architect is from Brazilian modernist architecture and its symptomatic structural showboating. This distance is precisely what enables Bucci, while employing typically Brazilian architectural themes and structural devices, to invest where our architecture had advanced the least – namely, spatial research.

In fact, Brazil's modern architecture has always been far more objectual than spatial oriented, more about construction than about voids, more iconic than phenomenological.[5] Hence Giulio Carlo Argan's claim from the early 1950s that this architecture relied excessively on the combination of technique and beauty – and precisely for that reason, also on an overly objectual, contemplative, classical notion of beauty.[6] Paulo Mendes da Rocha's specific contribution to Brazil's architecture resides, from that perspective, on the attention he gives to the void.[7]

BUCCI, HOWEVER, DOES NOT SEEM CONTENT – NOT ANYMORE, ANYWAY – IN PICKING UP FROM WHERE MENDES DA ROCHA HAD STOPPED. HIS STARTING POINT IS NOT EVEN ARTIGAS. HE FEELS ENTITLED, PERHAPS EVEN OBLIGED, TO GO ALL THE WAY BACK TO REIDY AND NIEMEYER. WHICH MEANS TO SAY TO LE CORBUSIER.

The confrontation between the East Hampton house and Casa das Canoas is enlightening. I said before that unlike what happens with the Niemeyer house, in Bucci's project plastic freedom is not ascribed to the roof slab, but rather to the basement. The formulation is imprecise. I would do better to state that unlike Niemeyer, freedom is not in the air, but on the ground. This is a radical inversion.

In the capacity of leading Brazilian modern designer, Niemeyer was much too focused on the task of demonstrating how vigorous our architecture was, especially with regard to structure. Each new project was therefore matched by a strict requirement – namely, demonstrating how innovative and, especially, how structurally virile Brazilian architecture was. Niemeyer's architecture has in fact always been doubly monumental – both in the sense of a landmark that celebrates a historic feat (i.e. the miraculous fulfillment of our modernization);[8] and in the sense of an object that elevates itself from the ground and, in reaching out into the air, stands out in the landscape – preferably against a free, unimpeded horizon. Put differently, his was an architecture that always conceived of space as a surrounding void, whose main function is to favor the contemplation of a monumental object.

Bucci, on the contrary, is particularly challenged by spatial research; the enormous attention he imparts to the design of the ground is an expression of that. He knows that walking is an activity forever tied to the shape of the ground; that, as per the teachings of Le Corbusier, "the plan is a generator. The plan holds in itself the essence of sensation."[9] Though formally freer, his floor designs aren't random, let alone purposeless. They reflect not only the corbusian premise that life is walking, and

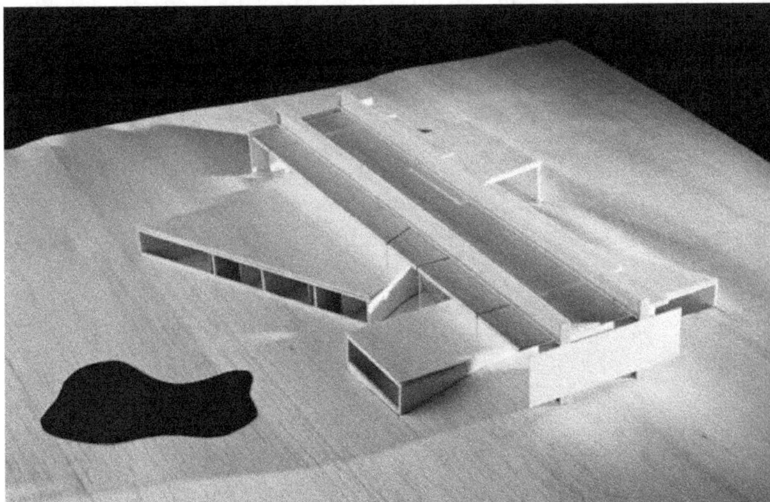

House in East Hampton, model, East Hampton NY. Angelo Bucci, 2007-2008. Photo Nelson Kon

space a construction that takes place in lifeworld, but also the understanding that walking always implies choosing between an objective trajectory and simply wandering.

Thus, there is no reason at all to match up the designs of floor slabs and structure. On the contrary: While a total disconnection (as in the East Hampton house) may not always be the case, it is at any rate important to make explicit that these are separate instances (and not by chance, as a rule of thumb, Bucci's covering slabs are not accessible to the public). This contrast is indeed emphasized through design: If primary structure and roof slabs are oftentimes

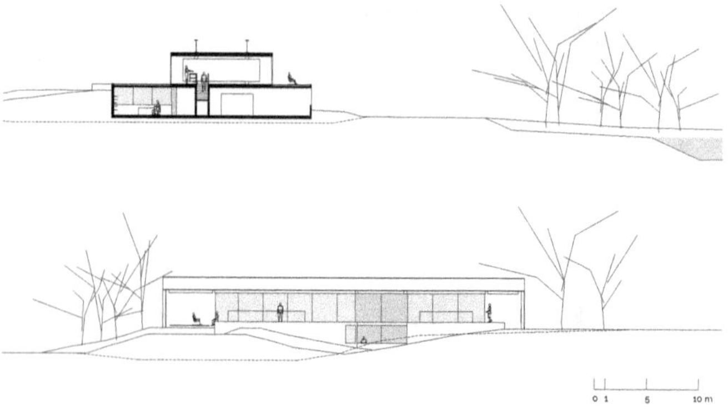

House in East Hampton, transversal section and elevation, East Hampton NY. Angelo Bucci, 2007-2008. SPBR Arquitetos Collection

orthogonal and rectangular, the geometry of floor slabs is usually freer and uncertain.

The Cotia house exemplifies that principle. A superstructure composed of two robust pillars and four large articulated inverted beams supports two slabs – a roof slab and a floor one. The roof slab runs flush with the main beams; the floor slab hangs from it. The contrast between both designs is unambiguous. Whereas the roof slab tends to fall in line with the rectangular beamwork design, never surpassing its limits, the floor slab frankly exceeds the projection of the roof slab, at once causing space to overflow and eroding the volume-object integrity. The plan for an apartment building in Lugano, Switzerland attests that the possibilities of that principle are far from depleted. On the other hand, the Church of the Nativity suggests that something gets lost when the opposition is diluted.

As in Carapicuíba, Bucci combines in Cotia two recurrent structural gestures in Brazilian architecture – one more closely associated with Oscar Niemeyer, the other with Affonso Reidy. And again, I believe the project's interest lies in causing the spaces that one and the other gestures generate to collide. But clearly there is another modernist master involved in both projects (and not in these two alone), namely the landscape architect

Roberto Burle Marx. There is no reason for surprise. For if, as I believe, one of the trademarks of Bucci's spatial research is the attention he gives to the design of the ground, it is only natural to resort to the work of the chief designer of the Brazilian modernist ground.

From Burle Marx, Bucci inherits not only a certain graphic style (marked by the combination of line segments and curves) but also an inclination toward a picturesque approach to ground floor design – an approach I tend to associate with a desire to elevate floor design to the status that modernism has always ascribed to painting, and never to floor designs.

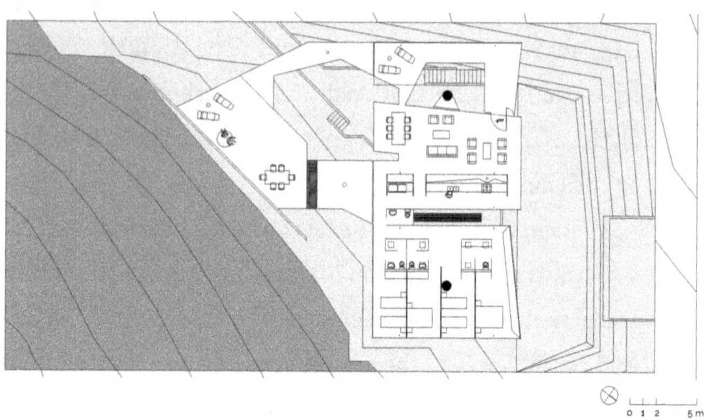

House in Cotia, living floor, Cotia SP. Angelo Bucci, 2008-2009.

SPBR Arquitetos Collection

ANGELO BUCCI

RISKY SPACE

And nothing seems more auspicious to me than the attempted coexistence of these three modernist masters – Niemeyer, Reidy and Burle Marx – in the work of a young contemporary architect such as Angelo Bucci. For as many Brazilian architects are aware, Niemeyer's relationships with the latter two were always tense, and occasionally outright conflicted. I am not referring to the realm of personal relationships alone – to the resentment that the episode of the CTA competition in São José dos Campos, won by Niemeyer, bred in Reidy (an episode which, partly at least, explains Reidy's boycott of the Brasília competition, whose judge panel included Niemeyer); or the angry public breakup of Burle Marx and Niemeyer, as a consequence of Burle-Marx's critique of Niemeyer's proposition

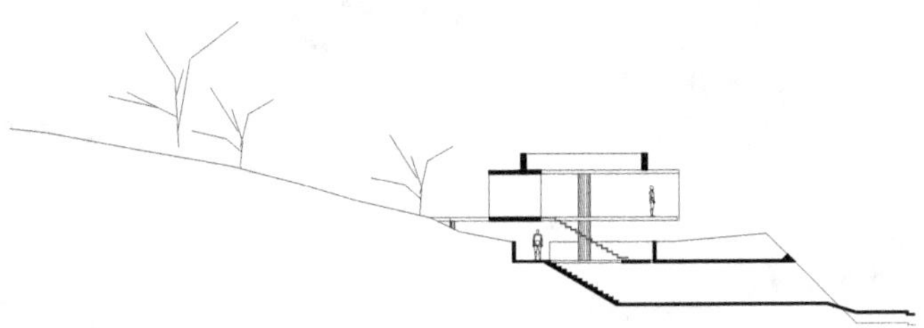

House in Cotia, transversal section, Cotia SP. Angelo Bucci, 2008-2009.

SPBR Arquitetos Collection

to build a monument in Parque do Flamengo. I refer to the idea
(which has prevailed in Brazil since Max Bill, in the early 1950s,
opposed Niemeyer's formal barbarism to Reidy's rigorous, rational constructivism)[10] that the architecture of these two master
of Brazilian modern architecture represented two antagonistic,
irreconcilable models – the first, associated with plastic freedom

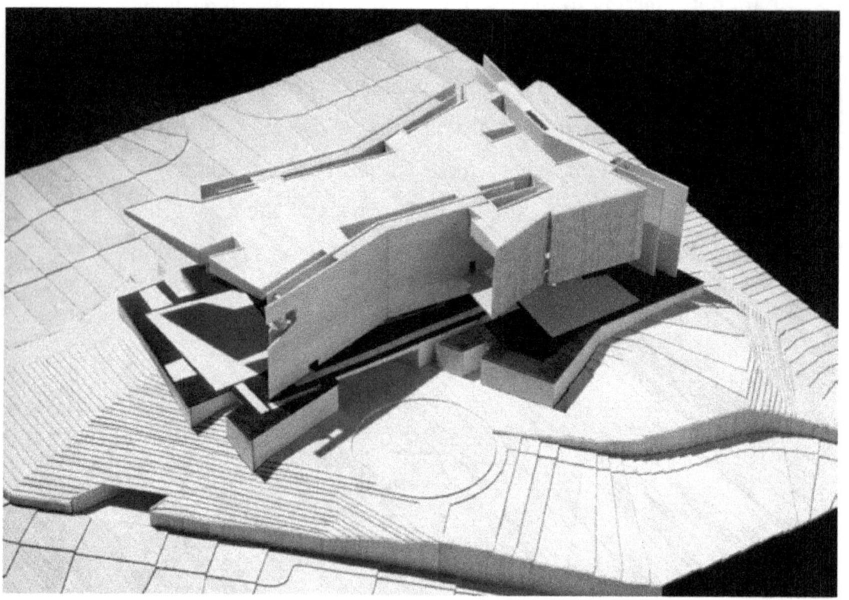

Natividade's Church, model, Culiacan MX. Angelo Bucci
and João Paulo M. de Faria, 2009. Photo Nelson Kon

(characteristic of Rio de Janeiro School), the second, with formal containment and constructivist rigor (characteristic of São Paulo School).

Subversively so, Bucci does not regard the works of Niemeyer (and Burle Marx) and Reidy as antagonistic, let alone irreconcilable. His démarche is not, however, merely conciliatory. On the contrary, it expresses the confidence that the juxtaposition of two, or better yet, three different approaches might eventually give place to an unusual, hybrid, impure – in a word, contemporary – development of Brazilian modern architecture. Needless to say how far removed he is from the mourners of modernism, with their nostalgic revivals. So if there is a lesson to be learned from his practice, it has to do with the ability to show that a productive relationship with the modernist tradition need be neither neo-modernist (that is, nostalgic, reverential, melancholic) nor postmodernist (through simple image quotation or linguistic deconstruction); that it can pertain to critical interpretation. Naturally, such an attitude implies assuming risks. How far is Bucci willing to go in this risky quest? We shall wait and see.

NOTES

EN. Article previous published at: Otavio Leonidio, "Espaço de risco/ Risky Space," *Monolito* 1, February/March 2011, 30-41.

1. Otavio Leonídio, "O túmulo do samba," *Projeto Design* 371, January 2011, 96-97.

2. The subject was approached in Renato Anelli, "O Museu de Arte de São Paulo: o museu transparente e a dessacralização da arte," *Arquitextos* 112-01, Vitruvius, September 2009, www.vitruvius.com.br/revistas/read/arquitextos/10.112/22.

3. Hugo Segawa, "Pavilhão do Brasil em Sevilha: deu em vão," *Projeto Design* 138, February 1991, 34-39.

4. The rationale borrows from the reading of Brazilian modern architecture which Sophia Silva Telles has delivered in multiple contexts.

5. The main reason for this is the fact that, like everything that descends from Mário de Andrade's brand of modernism, Brazilian architecture too had to be thematic, meaning that it had to adapt to the theme of Brazility. And, of course, it is much easier to thematize the visible (the built thing) than it is the invisible (the gap).

6. Giulio Carlo Argan, "Arquitetura moderna no Brasil," in *Depoimento de uma geração: arquitetura moderna brasileira*, ed. Alberto Xavier (São Paulo: Cosac Naify, 2003), 158-163.

7. Sophia Silva V. Telles, "Museu da Escultura visto por Sophia Telles," *AU – Arquitetura e Urbanismo* 32, October/November 1990.

ANGELO BUCCI

RISKY SPACE

8. Which makes our modern architecture totemic, more so than it is iconic.

9. Le Corbusier and Pierre Jeanneret, *Le Corbusier et Pierre Jeanneret – Oeuvre Complete 1910-1929* (Zurique: Les Éditions d'Architecture Erlenbarch, 1946), 33. The translation is mine.

10. Max Bill, "Max Bill critica a nossa moderna arquitetura," *Manchete* 60, June 13, 1953, 38-39.

CHRISTIAN DE PORTZAMPARC THE INVADER

TRANSLATED BY CARLOS EDUARDO DIAS COMAS

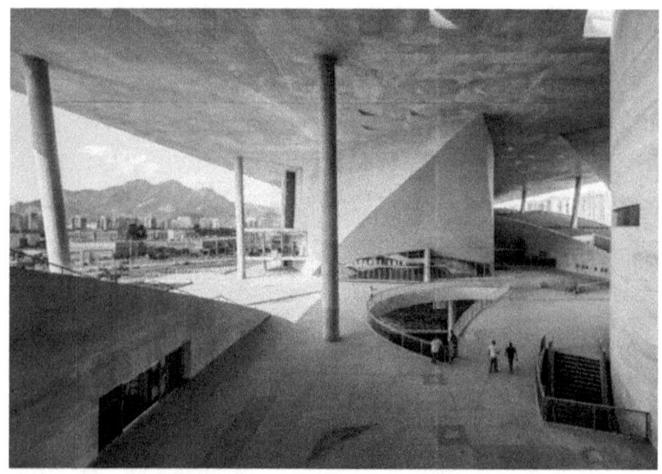

Cidade da Música, currently Cidade das Artes, Rio de Janeiro RJ.

Christian de Portzamparc, 2002-2013. Photo Nelson Kon

They say in Brazil that the form of the building is an echo of the
Brazilian architecture of the 1950s.

Christian de Portzamparc, *Filiations franco-brésiliennes*, 2006.

The acceleration of work on the construction site of Cidade da
Música [City of Music] found a curious parallel in the increasing
number of articles about this project in the local press. Unfortunately, nothing that has been written addresses the qualities (or
the eventual lack of qualities) of its design, signed by the French
architect Christian de Portzamparc (Casablanca, 1944). Led by
the newspaper *O Globo*, the local press approach to the construction of that large cultural ensemble follows a single point of
view, that of building cost or, more precisely, the fact that it far
surpasses the original budget. Of course these articles are not
signed by architects. As usual, they remain silent.[1]

Although predictable, the silence of the architectural
milieu is at once troubling and eloquent; after all, from the standpoint of Brazilian architecture this is not – or at least should
not be seen as – an ordinary project.

Brazilian architects like to think that, in contrast with
everything made in Brazil under the flag of modern art, Brazilian modern architecture was a true exceptional achievement, mainly due to its so celebrated international acceptance.

This is, at least, what we have been repeating since 1943, when the Museum of Modern Art of New York – MoMA supposedly surrendered to the force and originality of Brazil's new architecture.

We know today how much this perception owes to the ideas of the great champion of Brazilian modern architecture, Lúcio Costa (1902-1998). This phenomenon did not go unnoticed: Ever since the 1990s, Brazilian scholars have been proficient in identifying (and in some cases, denouncing) the *narrative fabric* or the *discoursive assemblage* of Brazilian modern architecture, pinpointing as a rule to Costa's utterances as the origin of this discoursive trope.[2]

On the other hand, Brazilian historiography seems to be aloof from another dimension of Brazilian modern architecture – namely, how the conception or image of this architecture marked countless European architects, in particular those who completed their studies throughout the 1960s.[3]

My own acknowledgement of these phenomena took place abroad, in the beginning of the 1990s, when I worked in the Parisian office of Christian de Portzamparc. I was struck at once by the constant mentions of Brazilian architects in that working place. Niemeyer, Reidy, Costa – these and other names filled our conversations and projects. And there were also names I had never heard of. I remember hearing about Bina Fonyat (an architect whose existence I simply ignored then) and how ashamed I was to say that I didn't know his design for the Castro Alves Theater, in Salvador. By that time Portzamparc traveled a lot to Brazil (almost always on vacation, with his Brazilian-born wife, the designer and architect Elizabeth de Portzamparc); each one of those trips was stamped by the enthusiastic discovery of a new feature of Brazilian architecture.

Later on, there was an episode that made a big impression on me, when, after two years at the office, I decided to leave France. The day I was going home, from a public phone in Charles de Gaulle Airport, I called Portzamparc. I felt uneasy and he certainly realized that; then, he told me something I will never forget:

You can be something I always wanted to be but I will never be able to: a Brazilian architect.[4]

That happened in March, 1993. Portzamparc was then 49 years old; he had not yet received the renowned Pritzker Prize but since the inauguration of his Cité de la Musique in Paris (1990) he was already well known outside France. Among other things, he belonged to a particular group of European architects – those who had intensely lived the 80s (that is, the overwhelming vogue of postmodernism) and now, in the beginning of the 90s, felt increasingly attracted by European architecture from the period between the World Wars and by Brazilian architecture from the 50s. So he belonged to the group (initially called *neo-moderns*) that, in the beginning of the 90s, started to rehabilitate the architecture of the modern movement.

Rem Koolhaas might be included in this group. In 1993 Koolhaas was not the celebrity he is nowadays; he hadn't published some of his most notorious texts (though his famous *Delirious New York* had already been published), and his ideas were just starting to gain the impact they have today in international debates.

But to me, Koolhaas was part of a special category of architects: Those who manifestly worshiped Brazilian modern architecture. After all, I had not forgotten what he said in an interview from the 1990s. Like Portzamparc, Koolhaas had an impossible dream to fulfill:

Until I was fourteen... I wanted to be some sort of Brazilian architect.[5]

As in most statements made by members of that group, the mood of Koolhaas' speech was confessional; one perceives in it a blend of melancholy and hope, as if a close affinity united his own youth to the naïf, wild, uncompromising force – to the freshness of Brazilian modern architecture.

Significantly, Koolhaas' discourse was essentially different from the one employed by members of the previous generation. To them, Brasília, especially, was everything but freshness, vitality, promise. On the contrary, it was a mistake, and might as well be considered a fraud, an attempt to cover up the background irrationality that characterized the process of modernity in general, and the modern movement in particular.

One of the characters of Simone de Beauvoir's novel *Les belles images* (a sort of quintessential European intellectual from the generation that preceded that of Portzamparc and Koolhaas), illustrates quite well this standpoint. To Alan Gilbert, after all, Brasília was tantamount to social exclusion; the city had not been made for those who had built it with their own hands. To live in the outer edge of the city, in wood shacks, was the only alternative left for them:

They had no choice... Rents in Brasília are way above their means.[6]

To the next generation, however, the experience – the adventure! – of Brazilian modern architecture might be seen and admired from a completely different point of view, and this notwithstanding the awareness of the social distresses inherent in its construction. In the words, once more, of Rem Koolhaas:

I think that Brasília has undoubtedly been the most accomplished statement about the modern city... just after Brasília's inauguration, it became evident that beyond Brasília there was another Brasília: that of the invaders. This fact has been told here in Europe to show the failure of the true Brasília. To me, what really mattered was the attempt.[7]

Brasília was inspiring not just for architects but also for future moviemakers. That was what the German moviemaker Wim Wenders, a contemporary of Portzamparc and Koolhaas, has recently admitted

My story with Brazil started when I was still a child. It didn't have anything to do with movies. I had a passion for Niemeyer and the idea of building a city in the middle of the jungle impressed me – at least that's how his work was then presented in Germany. On the wall of my room I gathered all information I could get about Brasília.[8]

I imagine that there is a whole constellation of European architects whose projects have the mark of Brazilian modern architecture. I can also imagine that, more than a specific repertoire, what marks their production is, say, the *spirit* of our architectural modernity – that which another foreigner, the North American anthropologist James Holston, called "the spirit of Brasília."[9]

If, as I believe, there is an interesting academic research to be done on this subject, Portzamparc's project is surely an extraordinary case study, and for several reasons. The first of them has to do with Portzamparc's nationality.

It is well known how dense the cultural relationships between Brazil and France are. When the French anthropologist Claude Lévi-Strauss came for the first time to Brazil, his goal was to produce an ethnology of indigenous peoples. However, what is interesting in his travel account, the book *Tristes trópicos* (*Sad Tropics*), is not just the study about the habits and mores of the Bororo. Equally interesting is the ethnography he makes of the Brazilian elite – an elite that adopted 19th century France as a model.

It is not surprising, therefore, that more or less at the same moment in which Lévi-Strauss took notes of the affinities which linked the Brazilian elite to a particularly literary French culture, Lúcio Costa (who, just like Affonso Eduardo Reidy, was born in France!) turns to France in his search for a guiding star to the new Brazilian architecture. The circumstances that resulted in the arrival of Le Corbusier in Brazil en 1936 are nowadays reasonably known.[10] We also know that it was thanks to Lúcio Costa that, as the historian Giulio Carlo Argan perceived, Brazil chose France in place of the German current of the modern movement as its chief reference.[11] Especially interesting, however, is to see how, in the sight of Costa, all the formation of Brazilian architecture might be interpreted in terms of an obligation towards France.

Significantly, it is to France that Costa turns to in 1951 when he feels safe enough to narrate the triumph of Brazilian modern architecture.[12] In Costa's personal view, such victory meant, above all, that the "debt owed to the old professor" had been "faithfully an honorably cleared after the completion of a century."[13] The old professor, in this case, was no other than Grandjean de Montigny, one of the stars of the so called French Mission, who, in the second quarter of the nineteenth century, brought formal architectural education to Brazil.

To Costa, one of the main achievements of Brazilian modern architecture was to fit in a tradition that included icons such as Grandjean de Montigny and Le Corbusier. Significantly, Costa always insisted that, despite being born in Swiss territory, Le Corbusier was, indeed, French.[14]

It is impossible to recall all the episodes that show the solidity and persistency of the relations between France and Brazil on the field of architecture. About the relationship Costa-

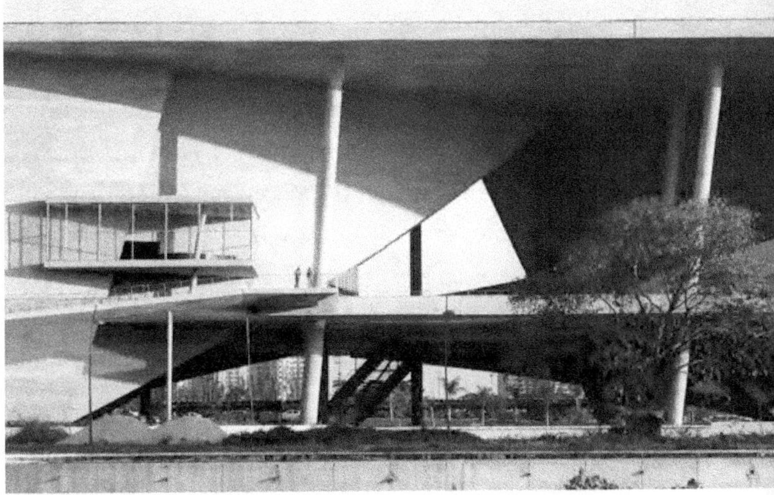

Cidade da Música, currently Cidade das Artes, Rio de Janeiro RJ. Christian de Portzamparc, 2002-2013. Photo Otavio Leonidio

Le Corbusier in particular, one should keep in mind that, when the French architect died in 1965, the transfer of his body from Roquebrune, where he died, to Paris was in charge of Lúcio Costa, and that the funeral's *décor*, which took place at the Court Carré of the Louvre's Palace, was conceived by Maria Elisa, Costa's daughter.

Forty years separate Le Corbusier's death from the design for Rio's City of Music. In the meantime, the bonds between French and Brazilian architectural milieus faded. A mutual indifference prevailed in many moments. During the 1960s and 70s French production was not too inspiring. Our own production did not arouse enthusiasm in France either. It was only after the renovation of the French architecture – which started in the first term of the Mitterrand administration – that a mutual interest would rise again.

However, it wasn't to Brazilian modern architecture that the new French generation turned to at that moment. If in Brazil postmodernists and critical-regionalists were gaining some influence (it is noteworthy that the present vogue of so-called São Paulo School had not started yet; the main star of Brazilian architecture at that point was Severiano Mário Porto), in France, besides Zanine,[15] the eyes were turned to… Niemeyer, Reidy, Costa.

The familiarity with Niemeyer (who had had an office in Paris, where he developed projects such as the headquarters of the French Communist Party) and the fact that he was not only alive but also working, may have been of help. Given the increasing dissatisfaction with the architecture produced in the 70s and the 80s (that is, postmodernist architecture), the good and old Niemeyerian architecture might as well be seen now less as a form of anachronism (or solipsism, or stubbornness, or ignorance, or self-sufficiency, or cantankerousness, or vulgarity) and more as evidence in favor of the idea of modernity as an unaccomplished project.[16] Of course, the overcoming of postmodernism undertaken by architects like Portzamparc did not imply a simple return to the modernist credo. Especially, his conception of the city was radically diverse from the most widespread version of modern urbanism – with its harsh rejection of traditional streets and blocks. In that sense, relinquishing postmodernism meant deepening the contemporary experience. An experience forged either by the perception of the limits of the modern movement, or a curiosity about its alternative meanings and its unexplored potentialities.

Even so (or just for this reason), numerous young architects in Europe had a growing interest for the old masters. I witnessed that when, in 1998, João Pedro Backheuser and me escorted Portzamparc in a visit to Niemeyer's office in Rio. It was an enlightening event. The French architect was visibly nervous; at last, he was going to meet the character who, as he told us, made him want to be an architect; he had brought with him a big monographic volume about his own work – a gift to the old master. The dedication had been written in Portuguese, and in it Portzamparc asserted that it was by looking at images of Niemeyer's buildings that he decided to study architecture – a statement he made public a few years later:

As numerous architects of my generation, I started to discover Brazil through the cinema and then through architecture, on photos and books, before even starting to study architecture. And it is through the images I saw of Niemeyer that I got the wish of becoming an architect like him.[17]

Since, clearly, he did not know Portzamparc's work, Niemeyer started to browse the book, quietly and bureaucratically. This didn't last long; for he soon remarked that between the forms of Portzamparc's architecture and his own work there was a striking resemblance. Then, staring at a photograph which featured a particularly Niemeyerian aspect of his colleague's work, he said emphatically:

– C'est beau ça! (This is beautiful!)

As expected, all Niemeyer could see in the works of Portzamparc was himself. But what has Portzamparc seen in the works of Niemeyer, Reidy, Costa? Above all, I think, a potentiality – as if the feats of that architecture might eventually give place to unexpected unfoldings. Which is why this building seems so didactical: It exemplifies a way of reprocessing a certain modern tradition. The extensive, laborious and exuberant use of reinforced concrete; the exaltation of the Brazilian *pilotis*; the exhortation of a culture of the shadow and, more broadly, of climate as a determinant factor of form; the adequacy to Lúcio Costa's Master Plan for Barra da Tijuca; the renewed bet on an architecture conceived according to the principles of compositional form; the belief in the emancipatory strength of beauty or, in Argan's terms, of the combinantion between technique and beauty – these and other factors indicate that, as in other projects, Portzamparc wanted and has been able to demonstrate, for the better or for the worse, what was still possible to do with a certain modern heritage.

From this, I believe, stems the uneasiness of Brazilian architects in dealing with this project. Because unlike Brazilian architects, Portzamparc does not feel intimidated by what

Abilio Guerra refered to as "the silent sphinx;" as a matter of fact, he seems entirely at ease with this tradition, to the point of even playing with it.[18] This easiness has an explanation: It is not just affinity but also estrangement what connects Christian de Portzamparc to Niemeyer, Reidy, Costa. Indeed, regardless of his esteem for our modern founding fathers, Portzamparc is aware that they belong in another time. More than temporal detachment, it is the perception of a crisis and the exhaustion (even if partial) of a program that which allows him to get closer to his modern heroes. The design of Rio's City of Music expresses that understanding: Brazilian modern architecture is on its horizon; but the awareness (in the case of Portzamparc, the personal experience) of the crisis of modernity prevents any illusion of a continuous and unproblematic fluidity between past and present. Brazilian modern architecture may be praised, quoted, paraphrased; but this will always be done from the perspective of alterity, not identity.

ONE UNDERSTANDS WHY PORTZAMPARC GOT SO NERVOUS WHEN HE FINALLY GOT TO SEE NIEMEYER. HE WAS NOT SIMPLY MEETING AN IDOL; HE WAS STANDING IN FRONT OF A GHOST.

The question that remains is: To what extent does this project partake in the strive for change and future-building intrinsic to the modern movement in general and to Brazilian modern architecture in particular? The question encompasses two others: Would it be desirable or justifiable to resort to modern aesthetics (its vocabulary and syntax, its spatial and formal devices) but at the same time remain indifferent to the issues in its origins?[19] Perchance are these issues amenable to being adapted to – local and international – contemporary realities?[20]

In that regard, one first observation: By all accounts, Portzamparc's project could not be further removed from the aspirations to social transformation that characterize the modern movement in architecture – in particular, its German branch. Or does anyone fancy its presence will even minimally transform social relations and living conditions of its visitors and neighbors?

To say that a project is devoid of social aspirations does not deny, however, its modern DNA – not necessarily, at least. For not all architecture produced under the flag of the modern movement intended to be – strictly speaking – socially transformative. One must not forget, after all, that a significant share of what was legitimately done in the name of modern architecture was, if not downright indifferent, at least critical to the notion of social transformation. This, by the way, was one of the essential, and most controversial, questions inherited from the debate of the avant-gardes of the beginning of the century – namely how to reconcile, on the one hand, the individual dimension of the experience of modern form and space, and on the other hand, the demand for universalization of that very experience. To Walter Gropius, the answer was to act upon the realm of production – not only through massification and standardization of an industrial output endowed with a new concept of quality, but also through the formation of artists who were artisans, and of artisans who were also artists. Le Corbusier, on the other hand, believed above all in the contagious power of good form; of a notion of beauty whose simple presence in the public space would suffice to move (and thereby transform) each and every individual who set eyes on it.

In light of that, it seems clear that Portzamparc's project share a strong conceptual affinity with the tradition of Brazilian modern architecture; and that the core element of such affinity, as one might expect, is Le Corbusier's understanding that "art must be brought to the individual."[21] Hence the significance of Lúcio Costa's early embracing of Le Corbusier's thinking as the theoretical landmark for the new Brazilian architecture: It provided the conceptual justification for an architecture which, from a conceptual standpoint, was not particularly focused on the social aspects of modernization, and which, for its bet on the individual, autonomous, and liberating experience of good form, was ethically allowed to be more individual than societal, more phenomenological than process-oriented, more concerned with creation, experience and presence than with production, development and progress.[22]

Viewed from this perspective, Rio's City of Music – with its bold, grandiose, disconcerting presence amidst Barra da Tijuca's postmodern landscape – somehow renews what is arguably the most outstanding feature of Brazilian modern architecture: Namely, the belief in the sublimation power of exceptional architectural objects amidst the space of the city. (Oddly enough, such feature renders this project at once more and less *Brazilian*. The timidity and diffidence that characterize contemporary architecture in Brazil are testament to the fact that, for good or for bad, new generations of Brazilian architects have altogether forgotten this feature of Brazilian modern production.)

Is this belief legitimate? Is there anything in the contemporary world to justify it? Someone with seventy years' worth of Brazilian modern architecture and fifty years' worth of Brasília under their belt will likely reply in the negative. Not that a significant share of that output wasn't truly exceptional. However, its effectiveness was and still is questionable: Apart from architects themselves (and not all of them), Brazilian modern architecture failed to sublimate more than a handful of sensitive souls (I meant to say artists, but the days when Brazilian artists followed what takes place in the realm of architecture are long past). Brasília, the corollary to the Brazilian modernist ideology, is there to prove it: The city where, in thesis, exceptional architecture would have bred a new experience of space and a new urban culture differs in nothing from any other Brazilian city. As is known, the city is maintained on a wing and a prayer by the pertinacious efforts of the National Institute of Historical and Artistic Heritage – IPHAN, and its average architecture is equal to or worse than Brazilian architecture in general.

BRASÍLIA, 'THE WORLD HERITAGE SITE' IS ALSO THE SAD, MONUMENTAL BURIAL SHROUD OF A MOVEMENT THAT PUT ALL ITS CHIPS ON THE SUBLIMATING POWER OF BEAUTY. IT MADE A BET AND IT LOST.

On the other hand, in a contemporary context like ours, where construction companies and their obscure architects provide Brazilian cities with as deplorable an image as one could fathom, it is hard not to be moved by the unexpected presence and the extraordinary beauty of Portzamparc's building. Its optimistic, courageous (and somewhat melancholic) presence gives it airs of an enclave, like a strategic bridgehead built in the war to regain a territory that had been lost to for a century now. Yes, half a century. Half a century of irrelevant, inexpressive, inconsistent, awkward, despicable, regrettable, unaccomplished projects. Are there exceptions? Of course there are. Has any of them, like this building (or Reidy's Pedregulho housing complex), truly left a positive mark on Rio's landscape? I don't think so.

Until very recently Brazilian architects kept asking themselves whatever happened to Brazilian modern architecture. Acknowledging the international inexpressiveness of contemporary Brazilian output, they struggled to understand how and when things got lost. Much more than a few linked it to the 1964 *coup d'étad*.

The Pritzker Prize given to Paulo Mendes da Rocha reinstated national self-esteem. Retrospectively, it was possible to recompose the lineage that links the golden era of Brazilian modern architecture and contemporary production (once again internationally valued). Starting from Lúcio Costa and

---

Niemeyer it is now possible to arrive – continuously, coherently – to Mendes da Rocha, passing by Reidy (seem now as a sort of fundamental link) and Artigas. Brazilian modern architecture has moved to São Paulo. It's all right. It is always Brazilian. It is always modern. It is always the same.

It is not surprising that in this grandiose, redemptory and atavistic tale, there should be no room for the invasive presence of Portzamparc's building.

NOTES

AN. This paper is based on the conference *The Troubling Beauty of Rio de Janeiro's City of Music*, presented at the Iberê Camargo Foundation, Porto Alegre, the 27th August, 2008, as part of de II DOCOMOMO-Sul Seminar. Many thanks to Carlos Eduardo Dias Comas for his comments on this essay

EN. Article previously published at: Otavio Leonidio, "Cidade da Música do Rio de Janeiro: a invasora," *Arquitextos* 111.01, Vitruvius, August 2009. www.vitruvius.com.br/revistas/read/arquitextos/10.111/32; Otavio Leonidio, "Cidade da Música do Rio de Janeiro: a invasora," *Arqtexto* 13, 2008, 122-135.

1. See Fernando Serapião, "A ópera do pequeno príncipe," *Piauí*, December 2008, 20-26. www.revistapiaui.com.br/edicao_27/artigo_835/A_opera_do_Pequeno_Principe.aspx; Ana Luiza Nobre, "Cidade da Música:

um lugar à sombra," *Minha Cidade* 104.03, Vitruvius, March 2009, www.vitruvius.com.br/revistas/read/minhacidade/09.104/1860.

2. Abilio Guerra, "Lúcio Costa, modernidade e tradição. Montagem discursiva da arquitetura moderna brasileira" (PhD diss., IFCH Unicamp, 2002); Carlos Alberto Ferreira Martins, "A constituição da trama historiográfica da arquitetura moderna brasileira," *Revista Pós*, 1995, 91-95.

3. About the place of that architecture in the historiography of modern architecture, see Nelci Tinem, *O alvo do olhar estrangeiro. O Brasil na historiografia da arquitetura moderna* (João Pessoa: Manufatura, 2002).

4. Otavio Leonidio, "Em Paris, chez Christian de Portzamparc. Geração Migrante – Depoimento 2," *Arquitextos* 030.02, Vitruvius, November 2002, www.vitruvius.com.br/revistas/read/arquitextos/03.030/729.

5. Rem Koolhaas, "Rem Koolhaas: de Brasília ao futuro," *Projeto* 133, 1990, 34-39.

6. Simone Beauvoir, *Les Belles Images* (Paris: Gallimard, 1966), 11.

7. Koolhaas, "Rem Koolhaas."

8. "Preciso filmar Brasília," *Folha de S.Paulo*, August 24, 2008, C12.

9. James Holston, "O espírito de Brasília," in *Um modo de ser moderno. Lúcio Costa e a crítica contemporânea*, ed. Roberto Conduru, Ana Luiza Nobre, João Masao Kamita and Otavio Leonidio (São Paulo: Cosac Naify, 2004), 159-177.

10. Maurício Lissovsky and Paulo Sérgio Moraes de Sá, *Colunas da educação: a construção do Ministério da Educação e Saúde* (Rio de

---

Janeiro: IPHAN, 1996); Cecília Rodrigues dos Santos, Margareth da Silva Pereira, Vasco Caldeiras da Silva and Romão Veriano da Silva Pereira, *Le Corbusier e o Brasil* (São Paulo: Tessela/Projeto, 1987).

11. Giulio Carlo Argan, "Arquitetura moderna no Brasil," *Comunità* 24, 1954, 48-52, quoted in *Depoimento de uma geração*, ed. Alberto Xavier (São Paulo: Cosac Naify, 2003), 174.

12. Carlos Alberto Ferreira Martins, "Arquitetura e Estado no Brasil. Elementos para uma análise da constituição do discurso moderno no Brasil. A obra de Lúcio Costa 1924-52" (master's thesis, FFLCH-USP, 1988), 169.

13. Lúcio Costa, *Arquitetura brasileira* (Rio de Janeiro: Serviço de Documentação do Ministério da Educação e Saúde, 1952).

14. Lúcio Costa, "Presença de Le Corbusier," in Lúcio Costa, *Lúcio Costa: registro de uma vivência* (São Paulo: Empresa das Artes, 1995).

15. Work that the Museum of Decorative Arts of Paris dedicates, in 1989, a retrospective titled *L'Architecture et la Forêt*.

16. Jurgen Habermas, "A modernidade como projeto inacabado," *Arte em Revista* 5, 1987.

17. Christian de Portzamparc, "Filiations franco-brésiliennes... Du Rio d'Agache à la Cidade da Música," in *Bresil France architectures*. Coleção Les Cahiers de la recherche architecturale et urbaine 18/19, ed. Philippe Panerai (Paris: Éditions du Patrimoine, 2006), 137.

18. Abilio Guerra, "A esfinge silenciosa," *Folha de S. Paulo/Jornal de*

Resenhas, June 12, 1999, 2.

19. T.J. Clark formulated this question in the following terms: "if I understand modernism to be a form of art somehow deeply attuned to certain facts and possibilities of modern life (of the form of life called modernity), then do I not think that the life we are living now is sufficiently different from that lived by Manet or Picasso or Pollock to deserve a new description – even if I may think it has not yet got one?" T.J. Clark, "Modernism, Postmodernism, and Steam," *October* 100, March 2002, 161.

20. Hans U. Gumbrecht, *Em 1926. Vivendo no limite do tempo* (Rio de Janeiro: Record, 1999), 317.

21. Le Corbusier, *A arte decorativa* (São Paulo: Martins Fontes, 1996), 189.

22. Otavio Leonidio, "Crítica e crise: Lúcio Costa e os limites do moderno," *Cadernos de Arquitetura e Urbanismo* 14, December 2006, 153.

ÁLVARO SIZA VIERA
ANOTHER VOID

TRANSLATED BY NICK RANDS

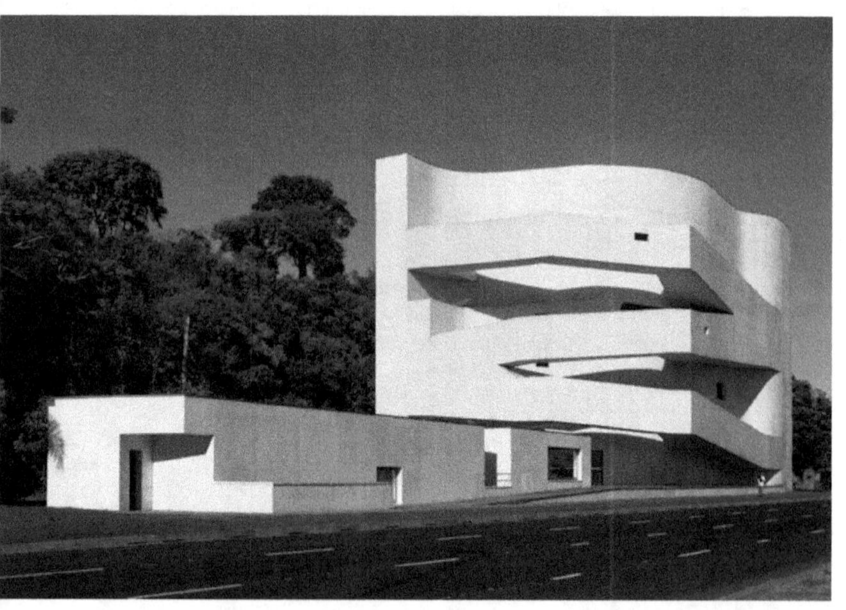

Iberê Camargo Foundation, Porto Alegre RS. Álvaro Siza Vieira, 2008.
Photo Nelson Kon

Navegar é preciso,

viver não é preciso.

Fernando Pessoa.

It has been said that the architecture of Álvaro Siza Viera owes much to the disquieting work of Adolf Loos.[1] It is not surprising, therefore, that one of the most recent and important buildings of the Portuguese architect, the Iberê Camargo Foundation in Porto Alegre (2008), confirms the enigmatic nature of his work.[2] But for the Brazilian public in particular, the unease brought about by an apparently indecipherable form seemed from the outset to be compensaded by a sensation of familiarity. It was, after all, not difficult to recognize from the initial images of the "Brazilian Siza" more or less explicit references to local modern architecture.[3] Can we not perhaps see in those reinforced concrete ramps (particularly the external cantilevered ramps protruding from the main body of the building) echoes of the structural prowesses and free gestures of the architecture of Oscar Niemeyer, Lina Bo Bardi, and the like? And yet, a visit to the completed building is enough to clarify how unfamiliar Siza's design really is.

The word *clarify* is not quite right, however. Despite the apparently photogenic nature of the Foundation building,

---

which comes across clearly enough in photographs, clarity is not one of the attributes of Siza's design.

Understandably, the building's most eloquent elements are the reinforced concrete cantilevered ramps that fly outside of the main body of the building. Siza obviously knows that external ramps rank among the elements most commonly identified with modern Brazilian architecture since at least since the 1939 (Brazilian Pavilion designed by Oscar Niemeyer and Lúcio Costa) for the International Exhibition of New York. The origin of this trope is hardly unknown. Costa, the great champion of modern architecture in Brazil, always emphasized that the unexpected and extraordinary blossoming of the local modern architecture was due to the "genuine seeds, planted here at the right time by Le Corbusier, in 1936."[4]

From direct contact with the French master, Brazilian architects learned more than how to employ the five points of a new architecture, how to take up the four basic compositional forms, and how to make use of the endless possibilities brought by the new technology of reinforced concrete. Above all, they learned "the undeniable foundation of all the plastic arts: *the forms that the eyes see*. Positive, objective attitude: clarity of reading; clarity of conception; *action*."[5] From which came the insistence on the "three reminders to architects":

1. Volume. Architecture is the masterful, correct and
magnificent play of volumes brought together in light.
2. Surface. A volume is enveloped by a surface, a surface
that is divided according to the generators and directing
vectors of the volume, accentuating the individuality of this
volume.
3. Plan. The plan is the generator. The plan carries within it
the essence of the sensation.[6]

But what sensation, exactly? As a product of the pictorial research of cubism, the sensation Le Corbusier spoke of was related to movement – the movement of a sensorial body in space and time. The complexity of his own work lay in the fact that it was at once idealistic – i.e. based on an unshakeable belief in the sublimating force of good form, classical and timeless – and anchored to a radical materiality.

According to Le Corbusier, the ultimate architectural experience – the ultimate sensation – would occur in movement, during which recognition (of classical form) and surprise (disco-very of the contingent) were combined to produce an awareness of form. The architectural sensation was, therefore, identified with the intelligibility of form, or rather with the process of the intelligibility of form – of clear form.

This was not, of course, a simple intelligibility. Le Corbusier's architecture proposed a play of spatial stratifications that implied "continuous fluctuations of interpretation," a kind of tension that, as Colin Rowe noted, always obliges viewers to produce new readings. Nevertheless, these stratifications never resulted in the dissolution of form.[7] On the contrary: despite its complexity, form remained intelligible to *the eyes that see*: "clarity of reading; clarity of conception; action."

Clarity is the crucial element in the Corbusian notion of *promenade architecturale*. It is not a random, arbitrary walk; on the contrary, it is an organized walk, predefined by a plan that resolutely establishes strategic and structural viewpoints – essential for a controlled fluctuation of meanings and interpretations – amidst a plurality of possible views.

Le Corbusier's architecture was cubist also in terms of its epistemological foundation, that is to say, in terms of a belief in: a) the essential clarity of language;[8] and b) in the innate capacity of *the eyes that see* to understand form by decoding the signs of that language. For Le Corbusier, the basis of this language was geometry – the sensorial mathematics that would visually translate the underlying universal order of contingent things.

While Niemeyer never adopted spatial stratifications such as Le Corbusier's, the spatial nature of his architecture was also

ÁLVARO SIZA VIEIRA

ANOTHER VOID

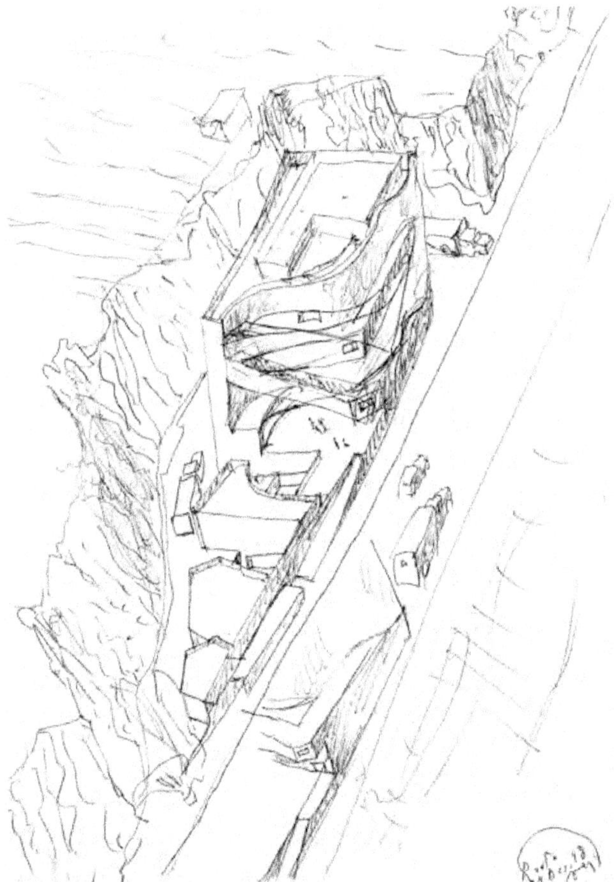

Iberê Camargo Foundation, croquis, Porto Alegre RS. Álvaro Siza

Vieira, 2008. Siza Vieira's Collection

a by-product of cubist research. Proof of that is his own use of the *promenade architecturale*. For Niemeyer, the *promenade architecturale* is almost always a device with more modest ends than it was for Le Corbusier; as a rule it simply frames one's perception of the formal integrity of pure volumes. In his most accomplished designs the *promenade* produces a dialogue between the formal integrity of pure volumes and the landscape in which they are placed. Conceived in this way, the Niemeyer *promenade* relied, as a rule, on one specific architectural element: the ramp – especially the curved ramp that rises to the entrance of the building and provides an overall view of it.

Niemeyer's insistence on the clear perception of the formal integrity of pure volumes explained his propensity to design curving ramps that start to rise from the ground floor well before engaging the building itself. Even when they do not allow for an overall view of the building (that is, the view from which the designer conceived the building), Niemeyer's ramps consistently emphasize the separation between user and building, or between the space surrounding the building and the space it contains. A Niemeyer building is thus seen to affirm its nature as object – as a pristine volume defined by a surface that envelops and contains it and whose internal spaces are separated from the outside by the plans of enclosure.

Another recurrent characteristic of Niemeyer's ramps aids in this process of objectification – namely the tendency to maintain a view of the horizon line. This perception of the horizon line, emphasized during the approach along the external, rising curved ramp, confirms to observers that what lies immediately before them is indeed an object – something that does not fuse (like in the architecture of Le Corbusier) with the space that surrounds it. This view of the horizon also enables one to situate oneself in relation to other identifiable and autonomous objects or bodies, which appear high or low, near or far, big or small. Thus for Niemeyer, more simply and directly than for Le Corbusier, the ramp is the element that enables a good reading of pure volumes. Ultimately, its specific function is, in fact, to clarify form and space.

But what about Siza's enclosed, cantilevered ramps at the Iberê Camargo Foundation? The first thing one notices about these ramps is that, once inside them, it becomes difficult to perceive the external space surrounding them. Contrary to what one expects when approaching the building – when one sees the ramps explicitly projected outward, suspended in air – when one enters these spaces, the sensations of externality and elevation simply disappear. As a result, there is a sense of frustration and incomprehension. What would be the purpose of all that structural effort if not to offer views?

A more detailed analysis of the spatial devices employed by Siza is enlightening. Upon entering the building, visitors are offered two main visiting routes: Either they can start the visit by ascending the ramp from the central atrium until reaching the fourth and highest floor; or they can take the elevator directly to the fourth floor and then use the ramp to descend to the ground floor.

At first, the design appears to follow a classic-modern spatial system, originally established by Frank Lloyd Wright for the Guggenheim Museum in New York. However, the experience of visiting Siza's building could not be more different from that of visiting the Guggenheim. For if, in Wright's case, the great central void never disappears from the visitor's vision, thus ensuring a constant perception of the whole, in Siza's case the opportunities for global views are intentionally restricted. The building's divided spatial system consists of at least three distinct entities: 1) the exhibition spaces themselves, located at the rear of the building; 2) the great void of the atrium in the central sector of the building, where the internal ramps of the museum can be found; 3) and the internal space of the cantilevered ramps that project outward from the front of the building. This system implies that, whether ascending or descending, one's movement will necessarily be characterized by the alternation of these three spatial conditions, each of which provides for very particular experiences.

The exhibition spaces, with their conventional geometry, are filled with the overwhelming presence of Iberê Camargo's paintings. Clearly, Siza had no intention of encouraging any confusion or intermingling between these spaces – with their conventional, almost monotonous geometry – and the central void of the atrium. The contiguity of these two conditions is controlled through a virtual vertical plan, defined by solid parapets that clearly separate one condition from the other.

The second spatial condition is the grand entrance atrium and the internal ramps that cross it. These ramps are characterized by the panoramic view they offer of both the atrium and the exhibition spaces. In contrast to the emphasis Siza gives to regularity and uniformity in the exhibition spaces, he reinforces the irregular and uneven aspect of the internal ramps: Here, parallelism, orthogonality, and planarity were explicitly avoided. Moreover, the full visibility of the atrium draws one's attention to the opposed yet complementary qualities of these two spatial conditions. Indeed, the unavoidable sight of the ramps on one side of the atrium accentuates one's perception of the diverse formal and spatial qualities of the galleries on the other side. The void of the atrium functions as an intermediary element that both separates and connects them.

The third spatial condition is the cantilevered exterior ramps. These are narrow, low-ceilinged spaces with strict thermal and acoustic insulation. Not a single picture hangs on their antiseptic white walls. A few tiny windows provide momentary and particularly unsatisfactory views to the outside. The number, position, and dimension of these windows are puzzling. So is their purpose: Are the windows there to punctuate the route? Or to allow strategic views of the landscape? Or just to let in some natural light? In any case, unlike in the galleries or the atrium, there is no visual connection with the internal museum spaces. This separation leads to an unexpected sensation of isolation.

It is a disturbing sensation. Not because of the isolation itself, but because of the disruption it subtly provokes. For despite everything we are forced to absorb from the moment we first see the building and the ramps projecting from its body, we feel as if we have somehow been led into a kind of illogical space, not only disconnected from the other spaces in the building but also released from its supposed spatial/structural logic.

THIS INTERRUPTION IS SYMPTOMATIC. IT DEMONSTRATE THAT THE DEFINING ASPECT OF SIZA'S DESIGN IS DISCONTINUITY, NOT CONTINUITY.

For Le Corbusier – in effect, for the most hegemonic, fundamentally constructive current of the modern movement – continuity was not just an important aspect of architectural design, it was one of the foundations (if not *the* foundation) of modern architecture's concept of experience. Continuity was emblematic of the connection of modern architecture with one of the central themes of scientific and philosophical thinking at the turn of century: The interdependence of vision, movement, and the content of consciousness. For authors as diverse as William James and Henri Bergson, the defining moment of the constituting consciousness occurred in a fusion of moments that always concluded with a synthesis of continuity and movement. For these thinkers, the formation of consciousness took place as in a film, in the form of an "integrated visual narrative" with its "taut stream of thematically connected images." The continuity of the visual experience unveiled the actual constituting consciousness – a process that revealed "the brain mechanisms that give coherence to perception."[9]

In this sense, the *promenade architecturale* was a device somewhat similar to the flow of consciousness – in the case of architecture, of the constructed consciousness of the architectural form. A consciousness that, immersed in the time and space of phenomenal reality, causes a kind of synthesis of sightings/experiences that are never really disconnected.

Ultimately, therefore, the *promenade architecturale* was not just *one* aspect of the Corbusian architectural experience, it was *the defining architectural experience*: The process – fluid, continual – through which the play of overlapping strata would be understood, articulated, and synthesized by vision (itself overvalued because of this), reaffirming the certainty – and the corresponding well-being – in the moving observer of the organic coherence of form.[10] The continuity of the architectural experience corresponded to the coherent and intrinsic unity of the form and thus to its clarity.

It is in this sense that the now-classic axiom "the plan is the generator" should be understood. For more than anything else, the Corbusian plan is the architectural apparatus *par excellence,* one that produced interdependent, yet fluid relationships between possible movements and necessary sightings. Like guidelines that structure the displacement inside his buildings, Corbusian plans are the synthesis of the twin conditions of consciousness – *coherence* and *fluidity* – signaling the penultimate clarity and intelligibility of architectural form.

Siza's plans, in turn, make clear that for him the defining aspect of the architectural experience is not continuity but discontinuity; that the continuous connection between movement and vision is not an essential condition for the organization of space. Eloquently, Siza's plans are made of disconected spaces, of formal articulations that are hidden, or imperceptible, to the eyes of the user – articulations that, in Corbusian terms, can only be considered abstract or unimportant, or at least negligible from the point of view of the visual structuring of form.

What these plans suggests, however, is that movement through Siza's buildings is often conceived as discontinuous and even disconnected; that the interruptions that characterize movement through several of his buildings are crucial for the definition of an alternative notion of an architectural experience – one that, not by chance, comprise decentering displacement and instability.

Here, Siza's affinities with Loos become evident. For as Frampton notes, "Loos was the only architect of the 1920s whose work was dadaist in feeling." dadaism was precisely the source of his "disjunctive conception of space," and his "perverse planning."[11] Commonly recognized as the theorist responsible for banishing ornament, Loos was also the designer who rejected modern movement's characteristic ideals of clarity, positivity, and externality; the architect who, shut indoors and protected from the light, investigated darkness, the discontinuous, and the enigmatic – the ghosts of modern, positivist rationality. The complex and disconnected interiors of his buildings, so often diverging from their external appearance, are evidence of this rejection.

Like Loos, Siza questioned the "hegemony of clarity." The enigmatic aspect of his buildings – their rigorous yet incongruous geometry, the disconcerting anthropomorphism of many of his facades, the abstract, even gratuitous geometry of these plans, the moving and often bizarre images that result from his designs, the recurrent "semantic disturbance" and "disjunctive repertoire" noted by Frampton – these are all aspects of an architectural aesthetics that from the outset never took continuity or clarity as its guiding principles.

In Porto Alegre, however, this approach seems to have reached a new stage, for the whole operation suggests an unprecedented commitment to opacity and discontinuity, the contradictory and the paradoxical. It is no accident that the highlight of this design is its cantilevered ramps, that is to say, the trademark of the radiant, positive, and transparent architecture of Le Corbusier and Niemeyer. The broad and unrestricted visibility of Siza's ramps is, in that sense, almost a provocation,[12] an indication of that vision – at least vision at the service of what Siza has called "inflexible knowledge"[13] – is not enough to address this opaque and paradoxical architecture; that for one to be able to do that one must bring imagination, reverie, and dreams. This is not to abandon visuality, but rather to recalibrate vision, so that it ceases to be a device wholly at the service of knowledge and become an instrument of the imagination[14] – the same imagination required when one confronts dada and surrealist objects.

It is not surprising, therefore, that this building should be endowed with characteristics more often found in objects by artists like Man Ray and Alberto Giacometti than in rationalist architecture or constructivist sculpture. In *Passages in Modern Sculpture*, the critic Rosalind Krauss describes some of those characteristics. "By being part of the real space and yet sectioned off from it," she writes, a work like Giacometti's *Suspended Ball* "attempts to open up a fissure in the continuous surface of reality." In doing so, the work explores "an experience we sometimes have in waking life, an experience of discontinuity between various pieces of the world." Surrealist objects are therefore far removed from the "constructivist resemblance between the rational object and the constituting consciousness." For "the constructivist relationship is predicated on the notion that there is a fundamental identity between the structure of subjective consciousness and the structure of objective reality."[15] The affinities between Siza's architecture and dada and surrealism also suggest why the emotion brought about by his building is similar to what one feels when viewing an object such as *Suspended Ball*: An emotion that, according to the critic Maurice Nadeau, is "in no sense one of satisfaction, but one of disturbance, like that imparted by the irritating awareness of failure."[16]

This affinity with surrealism explains why the windows, although they may be few and of insignificant size, have not simply been removed from the building's cantilevered ramps. The intended effect is not the total suppression of the outdoor view from inside, but the paradoxical and enigmatic coexistence (imposed despite objective vision) between internality and externality, between suspension and grounding, as if the void surrounding the ramps were also, somehow, a solid void.

This is not nonsense. For in a sense the cantilevered ramps are not just surrounded by the atmospheric void, which by definition is transparent and extendable; they are also surrounded by its ghost, the ghost of something that, in a perverse way, was not completely removed from their surrounding space.

Analysis of the plans, sections, and elevations allows one to see how, in Porto Alegre, Siza engages a semantic tension between the two essential elements of the formal structuring of his building – namely the plans that define the virtual rectangular block that envelops the building; and the curved plan that delimits and defines the void of the atrium and is expressed on the exterior. The concordance (the moment of co-planarity) between these two plans on the north facade demonstrates that their respective autonomy and independence are somehow incomplete. In fact, although the prevailing reciprocal distancing of the plans demonstrates physical independence, the moment of co-planarity seems to emphasize that the autonomy between the two plans is somehow precarious. The complexity of the operation lies in this underlying ambivalence. From the viewpoint of someone inside the exhibition spaces, or moving along the internal ramps of the museum, the curved plan that defines the void of the atrium is perceived as the plan that separates the inside from the outside of the building; it performs, therefore, the more or less conventional role of the "facade plan" – that is to say that which traditionally separates the inside from the outside of a building.

However, the internal route through the cantilevered ramps indicates that this reading is incomplete. Because what presented itself from the outset as pure exteriority is also experienced as an extreme form of interiority.

As we have seen, this feeling is caused by the absence of windows and, as a consequence, by the poor visibility to the exterior. But, as we now realize, that is not all. For the feeling of interiority also stems from the fact that, even as we know that we are walking inside a flying, protruded ramp, we are also aware that even at this point in the promenade we have never transposed the limits of the virtual block that envelops the building. In effect, even the idea that these are cantilevered ramps, protruding from the main body of the building, is problematic. And that is because the co-planarity that originates both plans has never been entirely dissolved.

A sequence of transversal sections demonstrates that the complexity and the spatial paradoxes of Siza's design derive from the dialectics established between, on the one hand, the physical separation of these two plans and, on the other hand, their virtual co-existence. The emphasis Siza gives to this dialectics (the accent given, in the north facade, to co-planarity; the simulation of the *real* collision between the covering plaster of the internal walls and the concrete

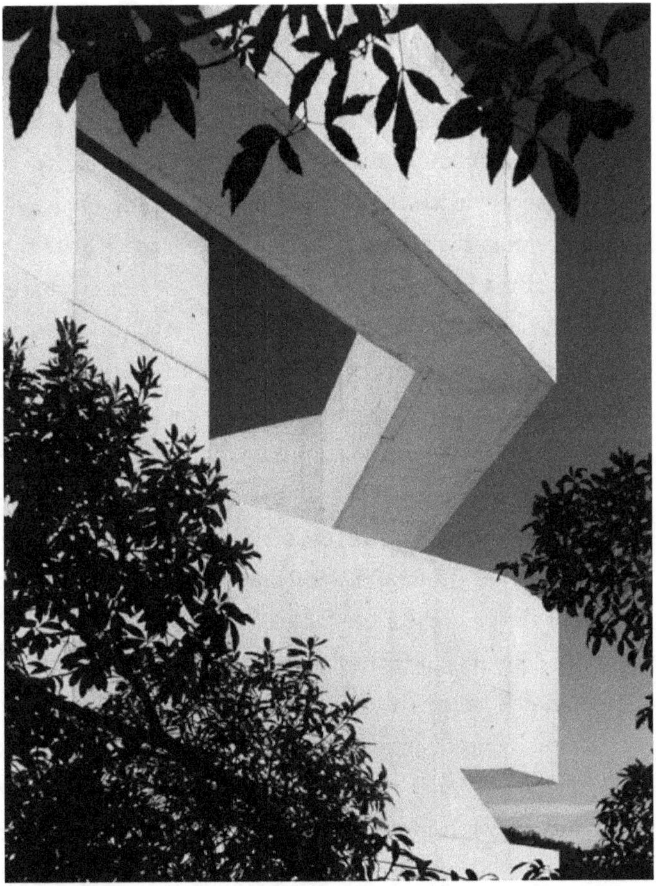

ÁLVARO SIZA VIEIRA

ANOTHER VOID

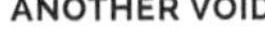

Iberê Camargo Foundation, Porto Alegre RS. Álvaro Siza Vieira, 2008.

Photo Nelson Kon

plans behind them; and, above all, the emphasis given to the collision of the ramp's interior with the exterior plan of the curved wall at the third floor) attests how this is in fact *the* crucial element of his design. The malaise one experiences whenever inside the flying ramps is a consequence of that. More than the physical devices employed to isolate the interior of the cantilevered ramps from the external spaces, this malaise derives from that essential ambiguity between the senses of autonomy and of indifference of this two plans – and even more so, from the feeling one has of being surreptitiously placed inside an intractable void, because it is also a solid one.[17]

Like the ghosts that inhabit Iberê's canvases, or the *ghostly agents* Frampton finds in Loos' works, the void between the virtual plan of the north facade and the curved plan that develops from it is the material that surrounds and supports Siza's extruded ramps. In a way, this is an illogical, absurd void – one that is radically different from the modern practical void, the function of which is to allow for full visibility and fluid continuity between inside and outside. (As Siza demonstrates the ghost of the void is not the solid, it is *another void*, transparent and yet opaque, empty and yet impenetrable, tangible and yet insurmountable.[18])

Siza's obsession with white concrete and the extraordinary efforts he employs to obtain it are eloquent. For if the Iberê Camargo Foundation has an allegorical aspect at all, its referent is the stone monolith – more specifically, the white marble block. In a perplexing and, unless I am mistaken, unprecedented gesture, Siza has challenged the impenetrable and intimidating solidity of the block of marble (the challenge it has represented, not necessarily for sculptors but for architects, builders of voids) and redefined the nature of the void within the realm of architecture.

But to speak of an allegorical image may be deceptive – and not because this design finds no place in the contemporary world of free circulation images. It simply finds its place in an openly subversive manner.

IN A WORLD WHERE THINGS ARE CONSTANTLY TRANSFORMED INTO IMAGES, SIZA HAS DEMONSTRATED THAT IT IS STILL POSSIBLE TO TRANSFORM IMAGES INTO THINGS.

Obviously, these will not be simple things, nor obvious, nor facile. But they will always be something more than mere images, and that is considerable.

And because it is more than an image, Siza's Iberê Camargo Foundation, unlike a large proportion of spectacular, photogenic, and tiresome contemporary buildings, is even more captivating on cloudy days than under blue skies. Dissolved in the mist, whispering that it also belongs to the realm of the invisible, it convinces us that, like life, architecture can be deceptive.

NOTES

EN. Article previously published at: Otavio Leonidio, "Álvaro Siza Vieira: outro vazio," *Noz* 4, 2010, 66-77; Otavio Leonidio, "Álvaro Siza Vieira: otro vacio," *Iluminaciones* 2, 2010, 53-63; Otavio Leonidio, "Álvaro Siza Vieira: outro vazio," *Arquitextos* 121.02, Vitruvius, June 2010, www.vitruvius. com.br/revistas/read/arquitextos/10.121/3439;OtavioLeonidio,"Álvaro Siza Vieira: Another Void," *Log* 16, 2009, 27-39; Otavio Leonidio, "Álvaro Siza Vieira: outro vazio," *Arquitectura* 21, January 1, 2010, 40-47.

1. Kenneth Frampton, "Álvaro Siza: Duarte House and the Teixeira Apartment," in *Labour, Work, and Architecture* (London: Phaidon, 2002), 299-303.

2. See Frampton, "In Spite of the Void: The Otherness of Adolf Loos," in *Labour* 197; and *GA Document*, Special Issue no. 3, Modern Architecture 1920-1945, 1987, 284.

3. See "Editorial," *Projeto Design* 341, July 2008, 49.

4. Lúcio Costa, "Carta depoimento," in *Lúcio Costa: sobre arquitetura* (Porto Alegre, CEUA, 1962), 124. Free translation.

5. Le Corbusier and Pierre Jeanneret, *Le Corbusier et Pierre Jeanneret: Oeuvre Complete 1910 – 1929* (Zurich: Les Éditions d'Architecture Erlenbarch, 1946), 33. Emphasis in original. English translation P. Morton Shand.

6. Le Corbusier, *Toward an Architecture*, trans. John Goodman (London: Frances Lincoln Publishers, 2008), 86-102.

7. Colin Rowe and Robert Slutsky, "Transparency: Literal and Phenomenal," in Colin Rowe, *The Mathematics of the Ideal Villa and Other Essays* (Cambridge: MIT Press, 1999), 159-184.

8. See Rosalind Krauss, "Notes on the Index: Part 1," in *The Originality of the Avant-garde and Other Modernist Myths* (Cambridge: MIT Press, 1986), 202.

9. Oliver Sacks, "The River of Consciousness," *New York Review of Books*, vol. 51, no. 1, January 15, 2004, 41-44.

10. On the process of autonomization of vision from the early decades of the 19th century, see Jonathan Crary, *Techniques of the Observer: On Vision and Modernity in the Nineteenth Century* (Cambridge: MIT Press, 1991).

11. Frampton, *GA Document*, Special Issue no. 3, 284.

12. That Siza's architecture operates with a vocabulary apparently identical to that used by modern masters (think of Oud, for example) is crucial in this sense, for it gives Siza's architecture a familiar character, locating it within a tradition by which he may amplify aspects of discord and irrationality.

13. Álvaro Siza, "Salvando las turbulencias: interview with Álvaro Siza," *El Croquis* 68-69, 1994, 6-31.

14. It can nevertheless be seen how the function of vision is redimensioned in Siza's work, which is no longer simply an organ at the service of knowledge, an instrument operating analytically in space as if comparing and reassessing operations put into practice by design devices, but an organ at the service of the imagination, reverie, or dreams.

15. Rosalind Krauss, "A Game Plan: The Terms of Surrealism," in *Passages in Modern Sculpture* (Cambridge: MIT Press, 1998), 110-114.

16. Maurice Nadeau, quoted in Krauss, 113.

17. Frampton remarks on some of the consequences of the play established between a "frontal plan" running parallel to the orthogonal grid of the exhibition spaces (an element that suggests the perception of the mass as an "eroded prismatic block") and the curved plan of the atrium. Frampton, "O museu como labirinto," in *Fundação Iberê Camargo*, ed. F. Kiefer (São Paulo: CosacNaify, 2008), 99.

18. Analyzing the *otherness* of Loos, Frampton also speaks about the *ghostly agents* present in his interiors. Referring to Loos's enigmatic penchant for a certain Egyptoid wooden tripod stool, Frampton writes,

ÁLVARO SIZA VIEIRA

ANOTHER VOID

"While their [the stools'] presence or absence may be entirely fortuitous, it is surely more than just another anomaly in what are otherwise seemingly innocuous environments. Perhaps we may see them as icons of a lost heroic culture sitting in judgment on an age, that in Loos's view, was totally deprived of any culture worthy of the name." Frampton, "In Spite of the Void," in *Labour, Work, and Architecture*, 203-204.

LELÉ
I LIVE IN AN ISLAND

TRANSLATED BY GIOVANA SANCHEZ AND OTAVIO LEONIDIO

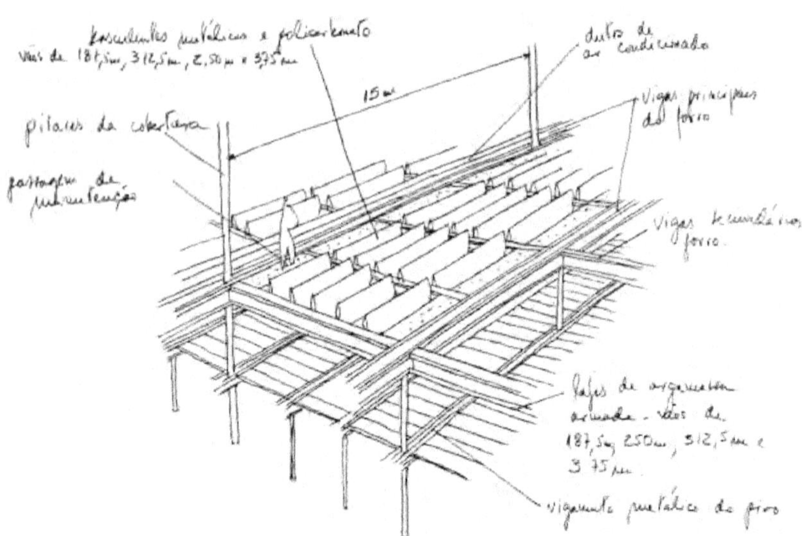

Sarah Rio Hospital, Rio de Janeiro RJ. João Filgueiras Lima, Lelé, 2009.

João Filgueiras Lima, Lelé Collection

INTRODUCTION

The recent death of Lelé puts an end to an exceptional career. Indeed, his oeuvre hardly fits into the profile outlined in the early 1930s by the chief ideologue of modern architecture in Brazil, Lúcio Costa, and personified in the 1940s and 50s by the works of Oscar Niemeyer and Affonso Eduardo Reidy.

Lelé didn't properly move away from these two characters; rather, he developed an original synthesis of their works, combining Niemeyer's flamboyant formalism and Reidy's rigorous constructivism.

The result of this combination is an awkward architecture. I say awkward due not only to the unusual form of Lelé's buildings, but mainly to the peculiar place his oeuvre occupies in the overall development of modern architecture in Brazil. More specifically, his work fits none of the two dominant trends that derive, respectively, from the works of Niemeyer and Reidy – so called *carioca* and *paulista* schools – the former extinct of now, the later more vibrant than ever.

The fact that Lelé had always repudiated (as stated below) this and other labels is twice symptomatic. On the one hand, it lays bare the mistrust he always had toward stringent critical and historiographical constructions. On the other hand, it indicates that if one such cleavage actually existed, its persistence could always be challenged.

What his oeuvre unveils, on that account, it is not so much the strenght of what he alone managed to accomplish as an architect (all the things that, as he himself admited, made him feel as though he lived in an island), but above all the unexplored possibilities inherent in the works of Niemeyer and Reidy.

The emphasis Lelé gives in what follows to the issue of training suggests that this, precisely, was the issue that mattered the most to him when, in October 2007, in the construction site of Sarah Hospital in Rio de Janeiro, he received me for this interview. On reading its transcripts on the day of his death (May 21st, 2014), it occurred to me that the island called Lelé might someday become an archipelago.

TRAINING

OTAVIO LEONIDIO: Lelé, how was your training as an architect?

JOÃO FILGUEIRAS LIMA, LELÉ: When I was in college, the school of architecture in Rio de Janeiro was still located inside the building of the School of Fine Arts. Funny, one would think that the School of Fine Arts would pay a greater attention to the artistic aspect of architecture – which of course it did – but there was also a very strong emphasis on technical knowledge. I remember, for example, that the courses on descriptive geometry, reinforced concrete, and strength of materials were considered extremely important at School. I had, indeed, a very strong training in structures and reinforced concrete – disciplines in charge at the time of professors Aderson Moreira da Rocha and Ademar Fonseca. Fonseca was even patron to my graduating class, so you see how much we acknowledged the quality of their teaching, how valued these courses were in school.

That said, I believe that also very important in my education was the time I spent in Brasília. Because soon after graduating, in 1956 (I graduated in 1955) when the construction of Brasília was still being discussed, I applied for a job there. Before heading there, I had a very rigorous training, thanks to the contact I had with Aldary Toledo. Toledo was a very learned man; he had worked with Jorge Machado Moreira and had a very solid cultural formation. He helped me a lot in this training period, when I was still in college. After that, the most important thing was to be in Brasília. Not from a humanistic or artistic standpoint, but from a technical one, due to the technical challenges one would face in Brasília's construction site. Because otherwise, it would never have been built. Strictly speaking, my role in Brasília was not properly the role of an architect. I made specifications for Superquadras [superblocks], and did the blueprints for Oscar Niemeyer's projects – which had to be followed quite strictly. Because of the conditions we found there, the construction site and the entire implementation of the work was very difficult. So this was a fundamental aspect in my training as an architect.

I would therefore highlight three fundamental moments in my training: the college years in Rio; working under Aldary Toledo, also in Rio; and finally moving to Brasília and having the chance to be in contact with Niemeyer – a relationship that was not to be restricted to that initial period but extended over many years.

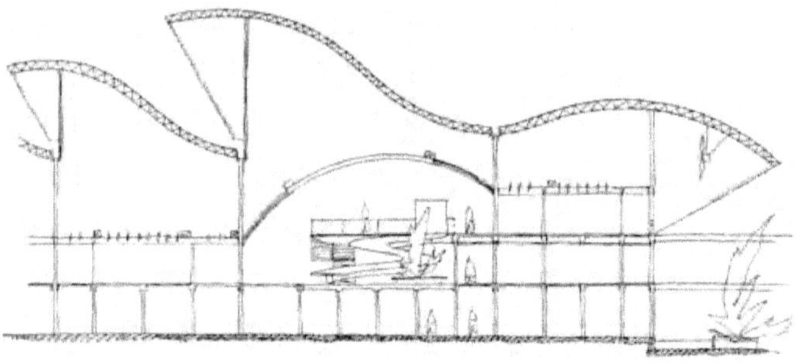

Sarah Rio Hospital, Rio de Janeiro RJ. João Filgueiras Lima, Lelé, 2009.
João Filgueiras Lima, Lelé Collection

OL: Regarding specifically the school of architecture you attended in the 1950s, was there at that point any connection between the artistic and the technical aspects of teaching?

JFL: I think this is a critical aspect in the training of architects – an aspect that needs to be constantly discussed: The increasing fragmentation of knowledge and the lack of integration between disciplines. Architects are by definition generalists, not specialists; either they are apt to communicate with all the involved experts, and supervise the entire work, or else they will inevitably lose control of the project. In this sense, the opportunity to work in Brasília was particularly important in my training. I had to learn very fast how to coordinate all kinds of additional projects.

Of course, there was a need for invention, and a degree of improvisation that oftentimes frightened me during my stay there. I had, as I said, a technical background, and I brought many books to Brasília (already imagining what I would deal with things I learned in school – foundations, for example). But in Brasília one would have to improvise. For example, there was no way we could wait for information coming from Rio, which only happened on Saturdays. It was once a week and that's it!

OL: And do you think you already had, at that time, a penchant for the technical, constructive aspects of architecture?

JFL: It's funny, I always thought that one's life is driven by chance. Brasília was an accident in my life. But one that drove me to a kind of work that, in time, I accepted – if not for the fact that I had not developed it by myself. For example, when I arrived at the University of Brasília – UnB, to work under Niemeyer, I had already some experience in construction, so I focused on the study of prefabrication, industrialization of components, etc. And then Darcy Ribeiro, the founder of UnB, who was an extremely imaginative and passionate man, suggested in 1962 that I should travel to Eastern Europe, in order to deepen my studies on the issue of industrialization in construction. Prefabrication had been much used in Europe after the War, due to the need for fast reconstruction, especially in housing. And it was very encouraged in the Soviet Union and Eastern Europe, regions that had been destroyed too. At the time, they employed in France a highly developed system, so-called Camus process, based on the use of load -bearing walls. But what interested me was not, say, the process itself; it was how prefabrication might be employed, the possibilities it opened. That, too, was a matter of chance: Darcy Ribeiro, who was always looking for funding, learned about a huge sale of coffee to Poland, and that as consequence there might be resources available there. So he foresaw the possibility of transforming this credit into resources for the University of Brasília. We then went to Poland, not just architects but people from all areas. In my specific area (construction), there were two of us – Sabino Barroso and me. It was a long trip, which lasted for about three months. We visited several countries; for example, we spent a week in Germany, then we went to Czechoslovakia, from there to the Soviet Union. Czechoslovakia, for example, had a very sophisticated construction culture, with a peculiar type of prefabrication. After that, we also went to France. It was a very productive trip.

OL: Lúcio Costa used to say that you are the "missing element" in the development of modern architecture in Brazil. He said that your work was the link between Niemeyer's creativity and Brazil's ability to build. How do you see this synthesis between art and production in your work?

JFL: I need to say, first of all, that my work went through several phases. I believe that the current phase – working in Salvador in the plant of Rede Sarah [Sarah Network], which of course offers me every opportunity to do research – is much richer. This hospital here in Rio de Janeiro is the product of this opportunity – the opportunity to work with various technicians, in close contact with the production floor. Nowadays, when I think of a project, I do it from the outset in connection with all these people. So there is always the possibility of discussing important issues that are being addressed at any given time.

In this specific hospital here, for example, there was a serious challenge regarding drainage. The site is in a lowland and the amount of land that had to be displaced in order to higher the ground would be enormous and thus very expensive. We then started to work with the idea of a shallow lake, directly linked with the adjacent lagoon, so as to reduce the volume of land to be displaced. Now, to reach a solution as specific as this one, in a site as specific as this one, either you rely on experts – in this case, on drainage – or else you won't be able to accomplish the project. For once the *parti* is set up and the precise location of the building is chosen, it is very difficult to go back. So I think there are certain aspects that have to be defined in the early stages of the design process, aspects that cannot be postponed. For me, today – I mean, to be able to develop a project that complies with the concept of architecture I set to do here, one that makes use of all the resources provided by industrialization – it is imperative to rely on a sort of team knowledge.

PRACTICE AND TEACHING

OL: Would you say, on that account, that the idea of the architect as an isolated creator is a misinterpretation of the craft of architecture?

JFL: I think this goes for certain architects. Take, for instance, the work of Oscar Niemeyer: The instinctive trait of the great creator that he is – that's so powerful... His work is so powerful that he is entitled to work as lone creator. Now I see myself as a normal person, and as such I must seek the most appropriate ways for my work to become at least satisfactory. For me, Niemeyer is a genius, and geniuses have to be treated differently.

OL: Personally, Lelé, I think that one of the most interesting aspects of your concept of architecture is not to make a distinction between architecture as a work of art and architecture in general, or even between architecture and infrastructure. Would you agree with that?

JFL: I agree, and I think that in the future, due to the ongoing fragmentation of knowledge, either architects assume the role you refer to, or else the profession will no longer be considered to be relevant. In a certain way this is already going on, and I do not know how our profession will survive if architects act otherwise.

Our craft is in danger now, and this is a topic that I have been discussing a lot, especially in schools of architecture, with fellow teachers: the need to face this specific problem. The fragmentation of knowledge is increasing, and this is a tendency that technology is imposing on us. If architects – defined as team-coordinators, as

---

generalists – are not able to take a stand in regard to all areas of knowledge they are bound to coordinate, then they will disappear. In medicine this is happening today at all levels; the general practitioner is disappearing. Today even within certain specialties, there are sub-specialties being invented. With all this, what disappears is the individual. So I believe the problem does not affect architects only, it is a problem of mankind, one we must confront. In certain areas, areas in which generalists operate, such as architecture, professionals cannot escape what I believe is their vocation: Either they change now or they will perish. I do not know if I'm being too dramatic, but it is how I see the issue.

OL: By the way, although we cannot say that you have become a specialist, you have developed a tremendous expertise in some areas, for example in hospital design. The late architect Arthur Lício Pontual used to say that unlike experts, good architects were capable of tackling any kind of project after one or two months of study. Do you agree with that?

JFL: I agree, but only if the architect in question recognizes the importance of specific kinds of knowledge. Because otherwise he or she will inevitably fail. For architects to become competent, to be able to talk to all the technicians required today in the realm of construction, they need to speak specific languages; they must therefore have a general knowledge. It is this common knowledge that needs to be taught in schools. What is the range of the knowledge architects must have in the domain of structural calculation, plumbing, electrical installations to be able to speak the language of structural engineers, plumbers and electricians – to be apt to discuss with these professionals? If they are unable to do so, and knowing that these are indeed different languages, then they will become isolated, and architecture will become once again a solitary activity. So I think Pontual is right – although at the time he worked, in the 1960s and 1970s, the fragmentation of knowledge was not as pervasive as it is today. A "CAD monkey"... – for Christ sake, what is that!

OL: Do you think in that sense that the practice of architecture has changed much? How did you manage to adapt throughout almost 50 years of practice?

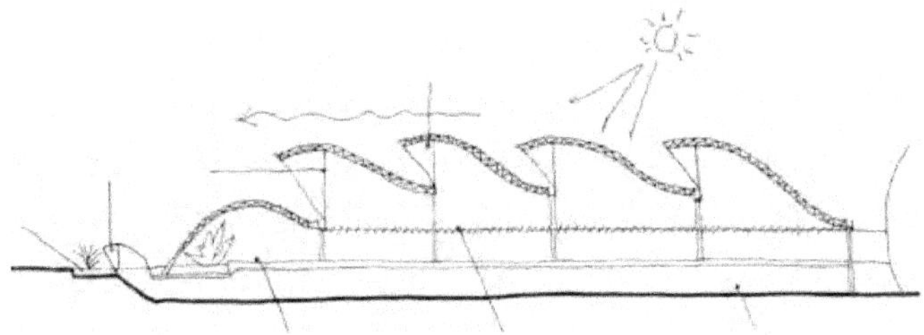

São Carlos General Hospital, São Carlos SP. João Filgueiras Lima, Lelé, 2004. João Filgueiras Lima, Lelé Collection

---

JFL: I think I live in an island, and therefore cannot generalize the experience that I have had, which is in fact quite unique. I do not quite know how practice is being carried out by fellow architects today. I think in Europe, in the big offices that I know, there is a tendency to have large structures. The offices of Norman Foster, Renzo Piano, and Santiago Calatrava are all super-organized and summarize this condition: They have a great structure, which is fundamental for the work they do. These are architects working with great professional integration. As for us here in Brazil, we are completely disintegrated. This is perhaps what's worse. In Europe they don't do architecture as we do it today in Brazil.

You have addressed the issue of hospital design: When I started studying hospitals, in 1969, I made a travel sponsored by the Government of the Federal District, with the purpose of visiting the most developed countries in this area (at that time, especially Nordic countries – Sweden , Denmark, Finland); and I visited several architectural firms. Well, in the medical field, in which complexity is much higher than in other areas, projects were developed with a great sense of integration in all areas of knowledge. Here in Brazil, if a firm is to design a hospital, it will receive a program that won't be even discussed – since this program will be treated as dogma. So there will be no contribution to the setting of the program – a program that you can be sure will have multiple problems. What, then, is the advantage of Sarah Network? The advantage is that we participate in the definition of the program, we discussed the program with physicians, with the nurses. Thus, treatments provided by Sarah hospitals are also defined by an architectural firm. That's why I say that my work today is an island, in a complex area such as hospitals.

OL: Regarding the programs architects are usually required to comply with, it is shocking how poorly thought they can in fact be. Wouldn't this be an important area of activity for architects – programming –, one that is still underexplored? Is it not the case for fighting for the expansion of an architect's scope of activity?

JFL: Of course! For example,

IN SALVADOR I WORKED A LOT IN THE FIELD OF

PUBLIC TRANSPORTATION AND SANITATION.

THESE ARE AREAS IN WHICH ARCHITECTS

SHOULD BE WORKING EXTENSIVELY, AREAS IN

WHICH THEY CAN CREATE NEW THINGS, MAKE

A SIGNIFICANT CONTRIBUTION.

Architects are purported to make contributions in these areas, and today we are not acting, not acting in any way…

OL: Why is that so? For a lack of political influence? Due to a possible weakening of the profession?

JFL: Today, architects are praised for exceptional works – for great masterpieces. These works became marketing instruments for tourism. Barcelona is a case in point. The architectural market is amazing. How much is invested in it! It turns out that this is an exceptional model, one that is not valid for the entire architectural metiér. Let me give an example: The other day, I received a student from Bahia, purported to be interested in discussing the program of a hospital. But when I tried to discuss the program of the hospital, she told me: "No, this program business does not interest me, I want to make a roof like Calatrava…" To which I replied, "But this is not a hospital. You can design a Calatrava roof, but don't call it a hospital…"

OL: The tendency of reducing architecture to images is intriguing because, on the one hand, architecture magazines are very important for the dissemination of architecture, but on the other hand there is a reduction to the imagetic aspect of a building, which is very harmful to architecture.

JFL: It is especially harmful to architectural education. If anything, it encourages one aspect of architecture, and those who are being trained will be strongly affected. I believe that the school is the place where this should be discussed, so that students are aware that there are other aspects, aspects that are much more important for an architect's routine.

OL: By the way, looking at the buildings you have designed, no matter how different the program, it is clear that some basic principles prevail, principles which always guide the design process – namely the principle of flexibility and extensibility; the principle of natural lighting and thermal and environmental comfort; and the principle of standardization of building components.

JFL: I think you just identified the three fundamental issues – those that have guided my work, especially in recent years.

OL: Abiding by these principles does not seem to inhibit your creativity...

JFL: On the contrary, I think it makes it richer. Take, for example, the issue of flexibility: Increasingly buildings become obsolete in a shorter period of time. If we do not think about flexibility and extensibility we will make buildings to last two or three years. This, unfortunately, is the state of architecture today. The buildings made today seem so permanent... As if a family's arrangement did not change every two years! I, for one, feel like moving to another house, another apartment, every three years, because I feel that my life – and the technology that enters my house – must change. In this sense, it's horrible to think of something so definitive. I abhor definitive and pretentious standards. The standard is, at best, a support for the development of your work. But it is horrible when the standard becomes a dogma. In a world as transitory as the one we live in, suddenly there is a rule which says that from now on you have to do things a certain way, that you can not change. That's terrible. Now we know that nothing is final. Much to the contratry, even human knowledge changes in one or two years. In the case of hospitals, it is a terrible thing, because the high-tech equipment (especially in the image area, MRI, for example), change every six months. In this case, if there is no flexibility, what do you do? One gets stuck with that equipment for the rest of one's life?

OL: Your work seems in line with several tenets of modern architecture. Do you feel particularly close to the architecture of Le Corbusier?

JFL: Very much so, not only me but my entire generation. At first I had some difficulty with the language, as we had to read all the books in French. But it was something I did: I studied all the work of Le Corbusier, each and every project. And I did it with the conviction that it was necessary. I learned a lot from Le Corbusier. I think that at the time of my training, because access was difficult, the information was more valuable. Today, access is very easy, you go online and get everything you want. So people do not filter the information. That is part of the challenges of today's education: How does one filter the information? Students should know that it is important, even today, to study the work of Le Corbusier. Until today, when I am practicing, there are many things that I still learn from Le Corbusier.

DESIGN, PLACE AND BRAZILIAN ARCHITECTURE

OL: Speaking specifically about your own design process, how important is drawing for you?

JFL: DRAWING IS FUNDAMENTAL. I BELONG TO A GENERATION THAT BECAME FAMILIAR WITH DRAWING SINCE SCHOOL. WITH THE COMPUTER, NEW GENERATIONS ARE LOSING A LOT OF THAT CONNECTION. I THINK THAT THE COMPUTER IS TERRIBLE BECAUSE YOU LOSE THE SENSE OF SCALE.

The monitor destroys the sense of scale. In traditional design, in perspective drawing, you are always aware of the scale. When I draw a perspective, I try to do it as accurately as possible. For a

---

long time I would do it this way: I would draw a perspective and then compared it with the actual building, to see how much had I eluded myself through the perspective. Drawing to me is a key instrument, because apart from being a supporting tool in the creative process, it provides a conviction that what I'm thinking is what I will actually get. It is a confirmation. Of course, the form is in your head, but the drawing is a way of anticipating the design. So without drawing I do not see how I could do a project.

OL: Is it true that drawing led you to architecture, because of the skill you had since childhood?

JFL: I still like to make freehand drawings. I loved and still do cartoons, motion drawings. I think it is essential. Look at Le Corbusier: His drawings are so rich, not just the architectural drawings. In the drawings for Chandigarh, for example, the lying cows, how beautiful they are! Le Corbusier wanted to capture what he saw. The whole experience in Africa – he sought to register it in drawings. Ronchamp, for example, has something of the M'Zab Valley, in the North African desert. It is a project that has been enriched by his drawings, with things he registered in his travels by drawing them.

OL: Did you used to sketch things that you saw?

JFL: I did, yes. Later when I worked in transportation projects in Bahia, I had a huge concern in reproducing historical buildings. I drew many of these things. I do not know if today students still do that but I remember that we had drawing classes outdoors. We used to go to the Public Promenade in Rio de Janeiro to draw, a practice that has enriched me so much…

OL: Another important feature in your career is itinerancy: You started in Rio de Janeiro, moved to Brasília, worked on the construction site of the new capital and then at UnB, then went to Salvador, where you returned to several occasions. You lived also in Abadiania, a small city in the state of Goiás, then returned to Rio to create the Schools Factory. How was it like working in places so different from each other?

JFL: It was very important, because one of the things that we are losing with globalization are local influences. In each of these occasions I was enriched, to the extent that I absorbed aspects of the local culture. And that ends up changing projects. For example, I recently did a project in Belém do Pará and another one in Macapá. The two projects are very similar, two hospitals, with absolutely identical programs. But I feel that the Macapá project is very different from the one in Belém. In both cases, I raised the ceilings, because of the heat, and the technical issues have been addressed much in the same way. But in both projects we see the marks of local inspiration. In both cases it was crucial to go and visit the site; see for example the precariousness and poverty of Macapá. Belém, in turn, has a strong historical context, with values that need to be integrated. For me, it is essential to know the place, conceive, for example, the site planning for each building.

One thing that I cherish a lot is site planning – a fundamental aspect of architecture. It is important to set up a relationship with the ground, something that must be intentional. People have lost the capacity to understand that kind of relationship. For example, Niemeyer's Contemporary Art Museum in Niterói is anchored to the ground, despite people saying that the building looks like a landed flying saucer. It is nothing like a landed flying saucer, the museum is super-anchored on the ground. The association Oscar sought is that of a tree rooted in the ground. In fact, he usually draws the museum as though it was a flower that sprouts from the ground. Now Oscar has other projects that seem to be resting upon the ground, looking as though they came from the sky and had just landed. Those are different conceptions. People seem to have lost the ability to recognize these things. The flying saucer aspect in the Niterói Museum in restricted to its circular shape.

OL: This is an example of the increasing inability to understand architecture in all its richness and complexity, don't you think?

JFL: This loss in perception is a tragedy. Things lose authenticity, the only thing that counts is the image. And the picture is driven by marketing. Everything is image. This is a tragedy for our profession.

OL: You worked with two of the leading stars of modern architecture in Brazil, Oscar Niemeyer and Lina Bo Bardi. How was it like working with them?

JFL: First, I want to say that in both cases, I always put myself in the position of a collaborator. I have not worked *with them*, I worked *for them*. Working around Lina was wonderful. Oscar is a friend I have, someone who influenced me the most, not only by his genius as an architect, but also as a great friend who has always been there for me. But Lina was also a good friend.

OL: was Lina very different from Niemeyer while working?

JFL: Although Niemeyer always worried about human issues, with which we have an obligation to be concerned, he was an architect! Lina was a different person; she was very involved with the artistic part of architecture. Besides, she had a strong character, sometimes even a bit violent. I remember that, sometimes, I went with her to meetings with the Historic Pre-servation staff (in Salvador) and it was always a mess. She was very outspoken; always spoke her mind with great forcefulness.

She was a frightening person. It was a picturesque side of Lina because, at the same time, she was a very sweet person.

OL: By the way, how do you see the separation made by critics and historians between so called Rio de Janeiro and São Paulo schools of architecture?

JFL: I do not make this distinction. I think that today, with its population, with so many job opportunities, São Paulo plays a very important role in the development of Brazilian architecture. In spite of everything, I think that's a key role. In this regard, Rio de Janeiro is a little behind today. Anyway, during the period of my education, Rio had great architects – the great Rio architects of the generation before mine. But I don't see two different schools. Today, for example, São Paulo has Paulo Mendes da Rocha – a great, very sensitive architect – one among many other architects whose work I greatly admire. They were preceded by Vilanova Artigas, who made a very important contribution to Brazilian architecture as well. But I see these works as adding up to one another. So I see no cleavage between São Paulo and Rio de Janeiro.

OL: From the standpoint of construction methods, you made a clear option for prefabrication. Why this choice of prefabrication?

JFL: I always worked in public projects, in the poorest settlements of Brazil, in the most vulnerable cities. In these areas, the demands are so great that unless you rely on industrialization, your goals would never be achieved. For example, in the domain of education in Rio de Janeiro, in the experience I had in so called School's Factory, it seems logical that if you rely on industrialization you will solve problems faster and with lower costs. My choice for industrialization happened because I needed to find solutions for social programs. Besides the prefabrication systems employed at the University of Brasília, my first big experience in industrialization was in Salvador. There, we started the great industrialization project with sanitation. That's when I started to work on a larger scale – because the city needed it. Because of the topography of Salvador, it was necessary to come up with alternative solutions, conventional drainage systems did not work there. In the case of the School's Factory, the initial program (following Darcy Ribeiro's characteristic enthusiasm) was to build 5,000 nurseries. If you do not stand with industrialization, that would be unfeasible. I still think, as we industrialize a number of things, that the same should happen in the domain of construction: It has to equip itself better. So we could respond to these demands.

OL: You once said, after 50 years of practice, you still learn a lot from your mistakes.

JFL: We learn a lot from each new project, and above all we learn from our mistakes. Errors make us suffer so much... I suffer so much with my errors. Just yesterday, I gave myself hell here. I did not sleep well tonight because of an error. Not exactly an error but the inability to foresee that what I had designed would be difficult to be built on site. It is not an intentional

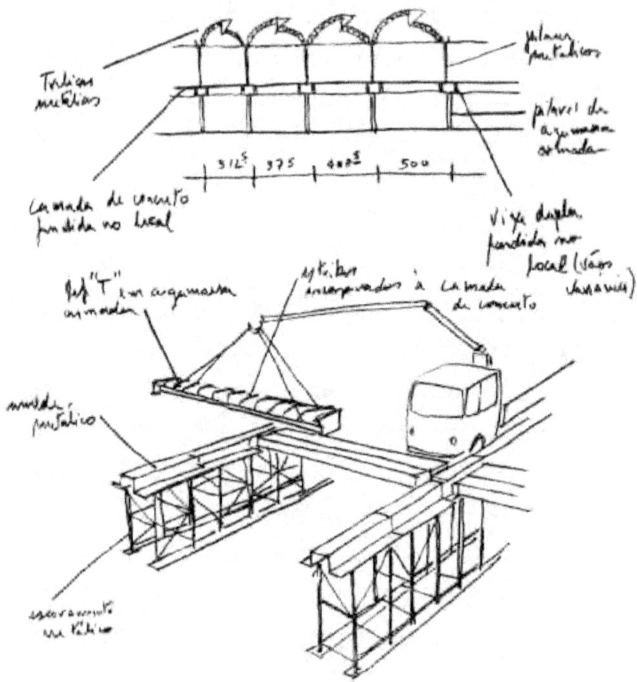

Sarah Recife Hospital, croqui of the prefabrication, Recife PE. João Filgueiras Lima, Lelé, 1995. João Filgueiras Lima, Lelé Collection

error, but a lack of experience. So every day is a new experience. Yesterday I learned something, as I do every day.

Now, when using recurrence – which is what we do in the factory – there is the opportunity of fixing errors and progressing. Recurrence is not mere repetition, is a form of improvement; it means re-examining an issue. Recurrence provides the opportunity to examine the error and improve upon it. So living with errors is for me a fundamental aspect of my work. Sometimes I want to redo a project only to correct the mistakes I've made. Because only when it is being built that you may look at what you've projected and say, "Wow, how much could have been better." So if you do not acknowledge all the mistakes you made...

NOTES

AN. The interview with João Filgueiras Lima took place at the construction site of the Sarah Hospital, Barra da Tijuca (Rio de Janeiro RJ) on October 18th, 2007.

EN. Article previously published at: Otavio Leonidio. "Eu vivo numa ilha. Entrevista com João Filgueiras Lima, Lelé," *Entrevista* 058.01, Vitruvius, May 2014. www.vitruvius.com.br/revistas/read/entrevista/15.058/5170.

LÚCIO COSTA CRITIQUE AND CRISIS

TRANSLATED BY LUCA SENISE

The Greatest quality of Gropius, for me the most important modern architect, comes from the awareness he has in his work… he never forgets the social significance of architecture.
Max Bill, *Manchete* 13, June 1953.

Sublimating oneself is a profoundly individual act.
Le Corbusier, *Precisions*, 1930.

OFTEN SEEN AS A PILLAR OF THE HISTORIOGRAPHY OF BRAZILIAN MODERN ARCHITECTURE,[1] "DEPOIMENTO DE UM ARQUITETO CARIOCA" [TESTIMONY OF AN ARCHITETCT FROM RIO] PUBLISHED IN JUNE 1951, differs significantly from Lúcio Costa's memorialist accounts of the mid- to late-1940s:[2] Instead of the past, Costa's "Testimony" aims at the future. While in the texts of 1945 and 1948 what was at stake was the setting of an authorized, unquestionable account of the rise and dominium of Brazil's new architecture, Costa's concern now was preventing that his creation lost its way.

Significantly, Costa did not associate such prospect to a purported disregard for so-called social aspects of architecture (as numerous critics, namely outside Brazil, had been claiming of late), but instead to the

latent disease we should fight, so that the work of true

architects do not get involved in the rising tide of artificiality

we now perceive specially outside Rio; [the] shiftless bastard

imitation characterized by the use of loose modernists recipes

unaccompanied of suitable plastic formulation and its proper

organic function; serious maladjustment [caused by] undue

interventions that we might call modernism pendants.[3]

But what would be the reasons and the basis of Costa's admonition?

Starting in the early 1950s, in parallel to the unprecedented and unexpected success of Brazilian modern

---

architecture,[4] a surge of critiques concerning its alleged formalism started to emerged, specially abroad.

According to the Italian critic and historian Giulio Carlo Argan, for example, although it was understandable – perhaps even justified – the initial choice Brazilian architects had made for Le Corbusier's conception of modern architecture, his option for technical formalism, it was time to start the "transition from an architecture that undoubtedly achieved a high level of quality to an urbanism from which one does not see except for some very early signs, yet pervasively oriented." From that moment on, Argan claimed, it was mandatory to

further the research about the social movements that, in Europe, determined the renewal of architectural forms; to go beyond what is nothing but a modern formal language; exceed the limits of an *art de luxe* that still makes the flourishing of Brazilian architecture the expression of a social elite. The urban problem is not just in what we might call *socialization* of such *art de luxe*; neither can it be solved in terms of the garden city and social housing complexes. Of course, the formula adopted by modern Brazilian architects can be further expanded, but it can never cover all aspects and problems of Brazilian society; it will always remain as the expression of a single class, regardless of their humanitarian interests in relation to the *lower* classes.[5]

Accordingly, Argan argued, the next step for Brazilian architecture would forcibly be "the inclusion in the building program of all the problems of a complex, not balanced or integrated society as is the case of Brazil."

A similar (if fairly more condescending) critique had been published roughly a year before by Mário Pedrosa – arguably Brazil's most influential critic. In his words,

Modern architecture radically presents the problem of urbanism, which in turn has not less radically presented the rational organization of the whole of society. The best of our architects today are increasingly aware of all these problems. Lúcio Costa, the veteran of architectural *modernism* among us, has expressed all these concerns when, in a recent article, argued for a new reconciliation between art and technology, for the benefit of the entire population. Unfortunately, we are still far from it. It should be recognized that our most beautiful achievements, our most beautiful palaces, are still an island in the country's immensity. Lúcio Costa himself recognizes the – very fastidious – fact that young Brazilian architecture is behind due to the overall development of Brazil. This creates an unfortunate gap between what is intended and what is possible and achievable. The most serious problem, popular housing, remains untouched. There are only outlines. In our first Architecture Biennale the international jury awarded the prize to A. Eduardo Reidy for the residential complex of Pedregulho. The jury found this beautiful realization of Reidy an example for Brazil because, through its bold solution in the field of housing, there was social improvement. A new path to achievement is open... But Pedregulho is still an isolated work: around it are the slums, shacks, the effervescence of poverty and chaotic form of urbanism.[6]

A third critique (arguably the most vehement among those addressed at the beginning of the 1950s to Brazilian architecture) came from the Swiss artist and architect Max Bill, and was uttered during his visit to Brazil in 1953. As highlighted by Nelci Tinem, Bill's criticism was part of a broader debate about Brazilian architecture's alleged formalism – a debate that involved characters as important as Walter Gropius, Ernesto Rogers, Giancarlo De Carlo and Sigfried Giedion. In Tinem's words, the debate reflected a "distrust about the future of a certain Brazilian production that emphasizes the visual qualities of the project."[7]

Unlike Argan and Pedrosa, Bill was unpitying with local architects. Claiming to know "almost everything so far published abroad about Brazilian architecture," he was in fact adamant:

Brazilian modern architecture suffers a little of this love for the useless, to the decorative. When designing, for example, the Pampulha buidlings, social function was not take into account. The feeling of human collectivity is then replaced by exaggerated individualism. The community is composed of individuals, but individualism destroys the community. Niemeyer, despite his obvious talent, designed by instinct, by a love for form qua form; he designed it around capricious free curves whose architectural sense is evident only for himself. The result is an excessive baroque style that does not belong to architecture nor to sculpture. I say, once again, that in architecture everything must have its logic, its immediate function. An architect should be able to defend the project even in its smallest details, and must be able to answer why he put a door in such place, why he painted such a wall blue, why he employed a certain type of window. The Greatest quality of Gropius, for me the most important modern architect, comes from the awareness he has in his work. He never discusses a project from the standpoint of any given style, he never forgets the social significance of architecture.[8]

But there was at least one Brazilian architect who seemed to contradict Bill's verdict: Affonso Eduardo Reidy. Asked about what would be, in his opinion, the best of Brazilian architects, Bill did not hesitate:

For me, the most important of all is Affonso Reidy, the author of Pedregulho Complex. I also appreciate the work of Lúcio Costa. However, when visiting the building that he designed at Parque Guinle, I could not help asking: "for whom was this building designed?" They replied that they were expensive apartments for the wealthy. I think it is a mistake to build only luxury buildings when there is a problem of public housing.[9]

Besides suggesting that the shortcomings of Brazilian architecture were the product of choices made back in the 1930s by its founding fathers, namely Lúcio Costa (who, quite expectedly, promptly went out to defend his comrades[10]), the critiques of Argan, Pedrosa and Bill have one more thing in common: They all take for granted that Brazilian architecture could no longer resign addressing "all the problems of a society" (Argan); proceeding to the "rational organization of the whole society" (Pedrosa); contemplating the "social importance of architecture" (Bill). That is, now that the initial fight had been won and an aesthetic hegemony was asserted, Brazilian architects could no longer avoid engaging in what these critics assumed was the ultimate purpose of modern architecture – namely, doing *social work*. How so? By generalizing modernity on a concrete, material level; by promoting the massification of modern buildings and the development of modern cities. As a legitimate descendent of constructivists avant-gardes, Brazilian architecture could no

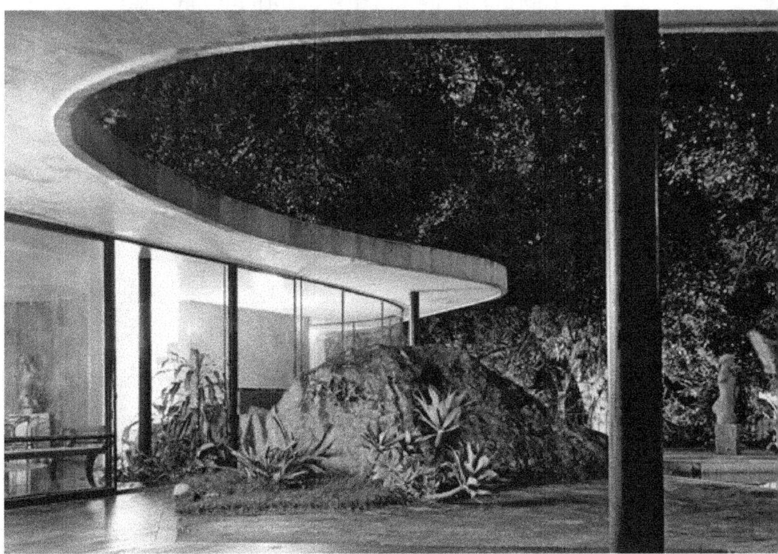

Canoas Houses, Rio de Janeiro RJ. Oscar Niemeyer, 1953/54.

Photo Nelson Kon

longer deviate from what seemed to be its logical development. Denying it would mean invalidating its very *raison-d'être*.

But something even more important underlies these claims, namely the idea that above all else modernity was a social process – one that, at least ideally, was apt to bring about economic development, social progress, collective well-being. Which explained the frustration that unfailing followed the perception of the gap that eventually emerged between modernity as idea (or as utopia) and the actual modernization of life, in its multiple domains – between what had been "planned" and what proved to be "achievable" (Pedrosa), between an *art de luxe* fitted to the needs of an elite and a social art that encompassed "all the problems of a society" (Argan).

Being truly modern (architecturally, but not only) implied, from that perspective, emphasizing modernity as a social process – either by joining it or, in the case of its absence, by struggling as hard as possible for its implementation. This was precisely the untold axiom of the critiques of Argan, Pedrosa and Bill: Ultimately there were simply no other parameters to appraise postwar architecture, Brazil's naive and flourishing new architecture included.

According to Costa, however, these one such conception ignored another crucial aspect of modernity, precisely the one upon which he had based his conception of a Brazilian modern architecture[11] – namely the autonomy of aesthetic experience, its ability to elevating its beholders upon the ordinary realms of existence, to giving access to a sublime aesthetic existence. And as he had learned from Le Corbusier's *oeuvre*, such existence was anything but collective; on the contrary, it was essentially personal. Understandably, Costa's conception of modern architecture was less concerned with the social aspects of modernity than it was with the notion of an individual, autonomous and emancipatory experience of autonomous forms in space. It was therefore more individual than societal, more phenomenological than processual, more concerned with creation, experience and presence than it was with production, development and progress.

Not coincidentally, Costa's model contradicted to the sociological bias of Brazil's avant-garde movements of the 1920s and 1930s.[12] These were in fact vanguards that always emphasized the sociological aspects of modern subjectivity, to the detriment of the individual ones. The tendency resulted in an obsession with sociological aspects of art, the main consequence of which being a prevalence of sociological representation over formal experimentation – as manifest for example, in Brazil's thematic literature and painting of the 1920s, 30s and 40s.[13] As

---

for Costa, he was more interested in a sphere of existence by definition extraneous to the sociological reality;

ONE POTENTIALLY APT TO RID INDIVIDUALS OF THE MULTIPLE CONSTRAINTS OF SOCIAL LIFE – NAMELY THE AUTONOMOUS SPHERE OF AESTHETIC EXPERIENCE.

Costa's fascination for this specific aspect of modern existence was made explicit in the early 1940s, when he sought to implement his most ambitious educational project – the attempted overhauling of the teaching of drawing in federal high schools. As his proposal makes clear, the pathway to a modern/aesthetical being-in-the-world depended merely on one's innate ability:

To see each form with its own character, as if we saw it for the first or the last time: ... a multitude of forms of diverse nature, rich forms of plastic content and well-defined configuration, although brokered at random and made by mundane objects: in the form of a cover on the chair, the form of a crumpled newspaper on the floor, the form of a corner of the sofa, the form of a pitcher, the form a coiled cat or a wallpaper *arabesc*;

and not only forms but also plans, for example, the meeting

of this wall with the floor and their relationship to the plans of

the table and the sofa; and yet colors: the blue of a faded shirt,

the *burnt-siena* complexion of a native, the clean yellow of new

blouse, various patches of gray against white or pink or ocher of

a whitewash.[14]

Not by accident, Costa belived that the ultimate task of truly modern architects (as opposed to "pendants of modernism," whose works unfailingly relied on "loose modernist recipes") was decrypting "the formal world not yet revealed."[15]

Now, the fact that Costa in 1951 vehemently repelled the charges made against Brazilian modern architecture suggests, I would argue, this: More than anything else, his goal was preventing that Brazilian modern architecture got involved – in the wake of critiques such as Argan, Pedrosa and Bill's – in what he saw as an inappropriate quarrel. It was urgent, therefore, to repel those accusations and pinpoint which, exactly, were the dangers that truly threatened Brazilian architecture.

Significantly, Costa's angry reply to Bill was based on the summary disqualification of the concept of community Bill employed in his argumentation (as per his definition, "the feeling of human collectivity is here replaced by exaggerated

---

individualism. The community is composed of individuals, but individualism destroys the community").[16] Costa's comment is, on that account, eloquent enough:

At one point, however, we are in full agreement. It is when [Bill] puts in evidence the splendid achievement of Pedregulho. But even here the ulterior motives of the critic are revealed when, in return, he discredits Pampulha. But without Pampulha, Brazilian architecture in its current form – Pedregulho included – would not exist. It was there that its distinguishing characteristics were defined. Indeed, the arguments brought up in the case are worthy of Beócia [land of ignorance in colloquial Portuguese]. It is a set of buildings designed for capitalist bourgeoisie – a casino, a yach-club, dance hall. Each was translated architecturally with its unmistakable character: the casino with its beautiful entrance, the wise connection of game rooms and theater, all touted masterfully; on the yach-club the extended pure lines; on the dance hall, the graceful moves that suits it so well. None of this fits into the narrow view of the Ulm master who lamented the individualistic spirit of the work – better say, the program – which does not correspond to the pure concept of collectivity, as if such a concept could only been expected from the down-to-earth.[17]

The question that arises at this point is whether Costa's urbanist experiences of the 1950s and 60s aimed at expanding to the scale of the city this conception of autonomous experience of modern form.[18] At any rate, one should resist assuming that underlying Costa's master plan for Brasília[19] is the desire for the total occupation of the country's territory by modern architecture (as envisioned by Argan, Bill and Pedrosa), as a model of what should be a truly modernized Brazil.

Evidence of that is the way Costa reacted to Brasília's unexpected urban development – in particular, the proliferation of so-called satellite-cities all around Plano Piloto. For many architects and intellectuals in Brazil, witnessing such process was at once painful and demoralizing. The experience was particularly hard on those who had believed in the transformative power (namely in the social transformative power) of modern architecture. As a rule, their reaction did not differ much from the way one of the protagonists of the novel *Les Belles Images* by Simone de Beauvoir: Just like Gilbert, they simply could not hide their malaise in the face of the evidence that Brasília was not made for those who had built it with their own hands. Living on the edge in wooden houses was the only alternative left for them, they thought. After all, as Gilbert stressed: "They had no choice... Rents in Brasília were far beyond their means."[20]

For this legion of Gilberts, the real Brasília was but the testimony of a gigantic and demoralizing failure. So all they could do now was acknowledging that failure, and denouncing the multiple contradictions, even the perversities inherent in the ideology of Brazilian modern architecture.

TO THE POPPING OF THESE CRITIQUES, HALF-HIDDEN IN HIS APARTMENT IN LEBLON, RIO DE JANEIRO, LÚCIO COSTA REACTED CALMLY. AS A MATTER OF FACT, HE SEEMED GENUINELY CURIOUS ABOUT WHAT WAS TAKING PLACE IN BRASÍLIA.

Indeed, the real Brasília differed quite a lot from the one he had planned. The central bus station, in particular (which was planned to give place to prosaic gatherings, in the manner of Picadilly Circus or the Champs Elysées), had been taken by hordes of commuters from satellite cities, in their daily march to Plano Piloto. Instead of petty-bourgeois discretion Costa had envisioned, the place had been stormed by a frantic, uncontrolled seethe of workers. It was like a shock of reality – a reality that had supplanted the dream.[21] But the reality did not bothered Costa, much to the contrary.

As for the dream... Well, as he had been arguing since the early 50s, it was a lot less ambitious and utopic than critics claimed it should had been.[22] And now, this proved to be quite an advantage. Not being conceived as an expressway towards enlightenment, industrialization, and social development, modernity was open to the unexpected. Not being a conviction to eternal hard labor,[23] it had also room for repose (so, *Riposatevi!*).[24] Life in Brasília wallowed in the petty reality of politics? Why not focus, then, in its exquisite, elevating forms – in the unprecedented spaces of Costa's master plan, the unsurpassed beauty of Niemeyer's palaces?[25] Were Brazilians actually "condemned to modernity" (as Mário Pedrosa had forecast)?[26] Possibly. But even if this was the case, there seemed to be alternatives left. If modernity in general was conceived as Brazilian modern architecture had been conceived by Lúcio Costa, then this might as well be a soft, light conviction.[27] It carried with it a sort of parole – one that could always be renewed. But for how long?

NOTES

AN. Article developed in the ambit of my PhD dissertation "Carradas de razões: Lúcio Costa e a arquitetura moderna brasileira (1924-1951)," defended at the Department of History at PUC-Rio in April 2005 under supervision of professor João Masao Kamita.

EN. Article previously published at: Otavio Leonidio, "Crítica e crise. Lúcio Costa e os limites do moderno," *Cadernos de Arquitetura e Urbanismo* 14, December 2006, 147-158.

1. Carlos Alberto Ferreira Martins, "Arquitetura e Estado no Brasil. Elementos para uma análise da constituição do discurso moderno no Brasil. A obra de Lúcio Costa 1924-52" (master's thesis, FFLCH-USP, 1988); Marcelo Puppi, *Por uma história não moderna da arquitetura brasileira: questões de historiografia* (Campinas: Pontes, 1998); Abilio Guerra, "Lúcio Costa: modernidade e tradição. Montagem discursiva da arquitetura moderna brasileira" (PhD diss., IFCH Unicamp, 2002).

2. Date of the inauguration of the building for the Brazilian Ministry of Education and Health. See Otília Beatriz Fiori Atantes, "Resumo de Lúcio Costa," *Folha de S. Paulo*, February 24, 2002, 6-11.

3. Lúcio Costa, *Lúcio Costa: sobre arquitetura*, ed. Alberto Xavier (Porto Alegre: Ceua/UFRGS, 1962), 198-199.

4. For the ones who shared such feeling the largest evidence of success was the unprecedented international interest about Brazilian architecture, visible in a series of publications and exhibitions, starting from the legendary *Brazil Builds*, organized by the Museum of Modern Art of New York in 1943. See Zilah Quazado-Deckker, *Brazil built: the architecture of modern movement in Brazil* (London/New York: Spon Press/Taylor & Francis Group, 2001).

5. Giulio Carlo Argan, "Arquitetura moderna no Brasil," *Comunità* 24,

1954, 48-52, quoted in *Depoimento de uma geração*, ed. Alberto Xavier (São Paulo: Cosac Naify, 2003), 174.

6. Mário Pedrosa, *Dos murais de Portinari aos espaços de Brasília* (São Paulo, Perspectiva, 1981), 261. The isolation of the MESP [Ministry of Education and Public Health] in relation to its surrounding was seen as necessary by Lúcio Costa. That's why we should distinguish between some exemplary operations and an eventual generalization of modern architecture.

7. In strict historiographic terms the text by Tinem (2006) adopts a revisionist perspective *vis-à-vis* the historiography of Brazilian modern architecture. Such is evident in statements like: "revisiting those documents shed some light in the comprehension of some blind spots of such canonical construction, contributes to understanding prejudices that erased or impeded some information, helps to understand the motives behind omissions as well as presences and celebrations, and supports the necessary overcome of presuppositions. Thus, it offers a small contribution to the difficult task of finding the main thread of an interactive narrative, unique and therefore fragile, signaling the importance of developing small parallel ropes that should avoid the collapse if the main artery burst, given how organic is the tissue with so many voids to be filled". Apart from that, I disagree with the thesis that the first texts by Costa correspond to a phase of "initial blindness, when the paradigmatic works had not yet been elected, nor had the

---

protagonists of such history, the architects that have not yet had the consciousness of their expression as a group". Nelci Tinem, "Arquitetura Moderna Brasileira: a imagem como texto," *Arquitextos* 072.02, May 2006, www.vitruvius.com.br/revistas/read/arquitextos/06.072/352. Free translation.

8. Max Bill, "Max Bill critica a nossa moderna arquitetura," *Manchete* 60, June 13, 1953, 38-39, quoted in *Arte concreta paulista: documentos*, ed. João Bandeira (São Paulo: Cosac Naify, 2002), 32-33.

9. Ibdi., 33.

10. Costa, *Lúcio Costa*, 252-259.

11. Otavio Leonidio, "Carradas de razão: Lúcio Costa e a arquitetura moderna brasileira (1924-1951)" (PhD diss., PUC-Rio, 2005).

12. Ricardo Benzaquen Araújo, "Introdução," in Ricardo Benzaquen Araújo, *Guerra e paz: casa grande & senzala e a obra de Gilberto Freire nos anos 30* (Rio de Janeiro: Editora 34, 1994).

13. Mário de Andrade stated that "sociology was the art of saving Brazil faster" (free translation). See Lucia Lippi Oliveira, "A institucionalização do ensino de ciências sociais," in: Helena Bomeny and Patrícia Birman, *As assim chamadas ciências sociais: formação do cientista social no Brasil* (Rio de Janeiro: UERJ/Relume Dumará, 1991), 53; Sérgio Buarque de Holanda, "Notas sobre o romance," in: Sérgio Buarque de Holanda, *Cobra de vidro* (São Paulo: Perspectiva, 1978), 62-64; Araújo, "Introdução," 20.

14. Lúcio Costa, "Carta depoimento," *O Jornal*, March 14, 1948, 56.

15. Costa, *Lúcio Costa*, 196.

16. Ferdinand Tonnies, *Community and society* (New York: Harper & Row, 1963).

17. Costa, *Lúcio Costa*, 258.

18. Le Corbusier, *Precisões. Sobre um estado presente da arquitetura e do urbanismo* (São Paulo: Cosac Naify, 2004), 84.

19. Lúcio Costa, "Brasília revisitada, 1985-1987: complementação, preservação, adensamento e expansão urbana," *Projeto* 100, June 1987, 115 and 122; Leonidio, "Carradas de razão."

20. Simone Beauvoir, *Les belles images* (Paris: Gallimard, 1966), 11.

21. Costa, "Brasília revisitada," 39.

22. Guilherme Wisnik, *Lúcio Costa* (São Paulo: Cosac Naify, 2001).

23. Le Corbusier, *Precisões*, 238.

24. Name of the Brazilian pavilion at Milano Trienalle 1964, designed by Costa. See Lúcio Costa, *Lúcio Costa: registro de uma vivência* (São Paulo: Empresa das Artes, 1995), 408-410; Wisnik, *Lúcio Costa*.

25. Interview with Tiago de Mello exhibited by GNT channel to commemorate the centennial of Lúcio Costa.

26. Famous summary of Mário Pedrosa.

27. The "light modernity" of Mammi. See Lorenzo Mammi, "Uma promessa ainda não cumprida," *Folha de S. Paulo*, December 10, 2000.

IN SEARCH FOR THE WORDS OF OUR MASTER

TRANSLATED BY LUCA SENISE AND FERNANDO LARA

THE RECENT PUBLICATION IN FACSIMILE VERSION OF 'LÚCIO COSTA: SOBRE ARQUITETURA' IS AN EXTRAORDINARY EDITORIAL EVENT, FOR SEVERAL REASONS. ORIGINALLY PUBLISHED IN 1962 BY THE ARCHITECTURE STUDENTS UNION AT THE UNIVERSITY OF RIO GRANDE DO SUL — UFRGS, THE BOOK WAS THE FIRST COLLECTION OF WRITINGS BY THE GREAT CHAMPION AND chief ideologue of modern architecture in Brazil – Lúcio Costa (1902-98).

Costa's contribution to the renewal of Brazilian architecture in the mid-1930s was indeed unparalleled. For example, the idea of inviting Le Corbusier to Rio de Janeiro, in 1936, and have him team-up with local architects for the design of the new building of the Ministry of Education – MES (a landmark of modern architecture in Brazil) was due entirely to Costa. Even more important perhaps, Costa would become since then the chief theoretician of, and main spokesperson for, the production that flourished all over the country in the wake of Le Corbusier's decisive stay. Justifiably so, when *Lúcio Costa: sobre arquitetura* was published in 1962, Costa – who was then 60 years old – enjoyed the prestige restricted to so-called great masters.

And it was in fact in search for the words of the eminent master that an undergraduate student of architecture, Alberto Xavier, began to collect a score of disperse and forgotten texts, some of which had been published back in the 1920s. As Xavier wrote in a note to the original edition, "a careful and patient effort to reconstitute all his works – which we saw as a true reliquary – seemed urgent for us."[1] Given the importance of these writings, it is indeed surprising that they had not been compiled until then, and that that this first collection should be

---

edited without Costa's knowledge. In a statement from 2002, Xavier recalled Costa's reaction when he finally learned about the publication:

One evening in 1962 I went up the elevators of the Ministry of Education in Rio and got to the seventh floor, were the headquarters of SPHAN [Brazil's National Institute of Historical and Artistic Heritage] were located. There, to make things easier, a prearranged reception team – sort of scouts – was waiting for me... They led me to Lúcio Costa's office – 'Dr. Lúcio's cave,' as it was known – and begin by saying, 'Look, Dr. Lúcio, some students are here...' They said it in the plural, repeating 'some students from Rio Grande do Sul brought a gift for you.' *Students* in the plural, so that I was not left alone; and *gift*, to mitigate a possible adverse reaction. Costa opened the book, surprised to see what was it about, looked at the his colleagues, looked at me, and said, 'This is a police matter!'[2]

Costa's reaction would seem enigmatic to the young Xavier,[3] but today, 45 years later, the reasons for his objections are fairly clear. After all, if there was something Costa had never resigned to was the control over his words – and not without a good reason. It was after all in direct association with his (remarkably effective) statements that the works of Oscar Nie-meyer, Affonso Eduardo Reidy, Jorge Machado Moreira and many others succeeded in asserting themselves as the authentic expression of so called Brazilian modern architecture, that is to say a distinctive and purportedly unforeseen version of modern architecture. Indeed, and thanks also to Costa's writings, such production appeared to meet the stringent aesthetic require-ments set up in the mid-1920s by the leading figures of Bra-zil's modernist movement, Mário de Andrade and Oswald de Andrade – a feat that no other artistic endeavor in Brazil came close to accomplishing. Understandably, such production would eventually be seen and praised, between the 1930s and 1950s, as an exceptional cultural product. This effectively gave Costa an unmatched public authority, of which he very soon became aware of, and to which he would periodically resort, consciously and strategically, choosing the themes and issues that should be addressed at specific moments, the fights he assumed were pertinent and opportune.

Now, the simple idea of the assembling – by a third party and without his consent – of so diverse and hetero-geneous set of texts would seem to Costa unreasonable and inappropriate. Unreasonable and inappropriate, it is clear, from the standpoint of someone who had been committed since the mid-40s to asserting an official memory of Brazilian modern architecture,[4] the meaning of which was to be asserted by Costa and Costa alone. According to Costa's reading, for example, the flourishing of modern architecture in Brazil, albeit surprising, was but the logical consequence of the first-hand contact he and his *protégés* had had in 1936 with Le Corbusier – an argument that, until today, is hardly ever questioned. Costa's awareness of the power of his statements would result in an exceptional caution with their usage – which excluded that they might be used, as it were, randomly or inadvertently. Now, this was exactly what Xavier did when he assembled *Lúcio Costa: sobre arquitetura*: a police matter!

AN ALTERNATIVE BOOK

And yet, this is precisely the reason why this book is so extraordinary. Not being compiled by Costa himself, the texts in question were not object to the rectifications (e.g. suppression of passages, altering of words and phrases, changes in the titles) Costa ended up doing to his written *oeuvre*.[5] The comparison with Costa's *magnum opus* – *Lúcio Costa: registro de uma vivência*, from 1995 – is in this sense revealing; it attests that Xavier's clandestine book is not properly a less comprehensive work but an alternative book, one that gives access to the original versions of texts that, as a rule, would be altered by Costa when he published *Registro de uma vivência*. Consider, for example, "Razões da nova arquitetura" (a touchstone of the historiography of modern architecture in Brazil) published by the prestigious *Revista de Engenharia do Distrito Federal* in January 1936: Among other changes, no less than four full paragraphs were suppressed in the version published in *Registro de uma vivência*.

The fact that these and other modifications have been overlooked by historiography suggest that some sort of critical shyness still prevails when it comes to addressing Costa's *oeuvre*. In effect, despite some rare academic studies,[6] Costa's written *oeuvre* is still read as per the script set up over the years by Costa himself. As is often the case, however (namely when it comes to public characters), such script is founded on the principle of biographical consistency. As a consequence, actions and statements carried out in specific contexts and for specific purposes end up being interpreted in terms of future events, and even more so in compliance with one's – purportedly cohesive and coherent – *thinking*. In Costa's specific case, many factors have contributed to this state of affairs, namely –

along with the obvious sophistication of Costa's formulations – a relentless effort to prevent that his own version of Brazilian modern architecture be confronted and eventually suplanted.[7] Which does not exempt Brazilian historians and critics from the task of challenging Costa's accounts, and addressing Costa's statements in terms of specific historical contexts, instead to simply corroborate the self-image disseminated by "Dr. Lúcio."

Viewed from that perspective, Costa didn't have much to complain about the selection made in 1962 (kept in the current issue) by Xavier. After all, and regardless of Xavier's original intention to make *Lúcio Costa: sobre arquitetura* as comprehensive a book as possible, the blanks that remained are substantial.[8] Indeed, thanks to the files made public by SPHAN, CPDOC (Research and Documentation Center at Getúlio Vargas Foundation), and the Le Corbusier Foundation; and thanks also to pioneering researches led by Lucia Gouvea Vieira and Maria Cristina Burlamaqui, Carlos Alberto Ferreira Martins, Maria Angélica da Silva, Cecilia Rodrigues dos Santos, Margareth da Silva Pereira, Vasco Caldeira and Romao da Silva Pereira, Mauricio Lissovsky and Paulo Sérgio Sá, Simon Schwartzman, Helena Bomeny and Vanda Ribeiro Costa, José Pessoa and Alberto Xavier himself, we know today that until 1962, the whole of Costa's written *oeuvre* exceeds 200 items, of which only 45 were published in *Lúcio Costa: sobre arquitetura*. Yet the problem is not one of quantity, but of selection. For the book does not reproduce some of the most important (especially from the standpoint of intellectual history) texts published by Costa in the 1920s and 1930s. The highlights here are the texts Costa published while he was still affiliated to so-called neo-colonial movement, as well as the ones he published right after breaking away from it and getting involved in a public controversy with its leader, José Marianno Filho. Now, the choice of not including these texts in the book (out of a dozen texts Costa published before 1931, *Lúcio Costa: sobre arquitetura* reproduces only one),[9] suggest a clear submission to Costa's autobiographical narrative – in particular, the emphasis it gives to the purported incompatibility between ideas previous to 1930 (understood as archaic) and the ones subsequent to that date (understood as modern). That this understanding prevailed during the editing of the book is confirmed by the list of works carried out by Costa until that moment, which makes no mention whatsoever to projects prior to 1931 – incidentally, the works that had made the fame of the young and prolific neo-colonial architect.

It is not surprising, therefore, that once the initial shock was over, Costa would soon realize that despite one or two potential sources of embarrassments (the worst, undoubtedly, his statement from 1929 that Aleijadinho[10] "had the spirit of a decorator and not of an architect," and that his work was never attuned to the general spirit of Brazilian architecture), Xavier's selection was entirely appropriate, and not at all "a police matter." As a matter of fact, apart from the text on Aleijadinho (which, as expected, was not included in *Registro de uma vivência*) all the book needed was a set of corrections and clarifications.

WRITING FOR POSTERITY

In this, precisely, lies the ultimate interest of the version being published now. For what had been reproduced in facsimile are not merely the original pages of *Lúcio Costa: sobre arquitetura*, but also the marginal notes that Costa added to the copy he received from Alberto Xavier hands in a distant and tense afternoon in 1962.[11] These marginal notes add an additional layer of meaning to the book; they provide a glimpse of what, in the eyes of the imminent master, deserved to be repaired; more importantly, they allow us to speculate about what, in each case, seemed to be at stake for him.

THE FIRST THING TO BE SAID ABOUT COSTA'S NOTES IS THAT, QUITE PREDICTABLY, THEY SEEMED TO HAVE BEEN WRITTEN NEITHER FOR COSTA HIMSELF NOR FOR ALBERTO XAVIER, BUT FOR POSTERITY.

I say predictably because at that point Costa was obviously aware that everything he wrote would gain at some point the status of a historical document and as such be the object of scrutiny and interpretation. It was important, thus, to set for the record that which, from the standpoint of an *unquestionable* reading, was not accurate or clear enough – so as to prevent the emergence of alternative, and eventually compromising, interpretations.

This becomes evident as one reads the marginal notes of *Lúcio Costa: sobre arquitetura* (made, presumably, in whole or in part, in 1966, since, on at least two occasions, Costa scored "30/I/66"). Basically, there are three kinds of notes: a) corrections or simple refutations of the original content of his texts; b) comments aimed at clarifying or complementing the original content of his texts; c) corrections of information provided by the editor, as well as complaints or reproaches about the way texts had been reproduced. In the first category, we may highlight the comments made to the text on Aleijadinho. Clearly,

Costa's purpose was to reiterate that ideas prior to 1930-31 were impertinent and not consistent with later formulations. One of these notes is eloquent enough; it reads:

Misconception. Wrong. Pure ignorance. I was exclusively

concerned with the beauty of the works of seventeenth and

early eighteenth centuries. I wasn't prepared to perceive the

highest quality of his work as an architect and as a sculptor.

In the second category are comments more or less clarifying, and some that seem simply prosaic. About the project for the University of Brazil (1936), Costa notes:

Splendid project. It is a pity that because of two lunatics – [Inácio

de] Amaral and [Ernesto] Souza Campos – the opportunity was

lost. Meanwhile, the incredible Fundão[12] drags on!

About "Ensino do desenho" (Costa's attempted overhauling of teaching of drawing in Brazil's junior high school) he writes, plaintively: "It is amazing how, a quarter of a century later, this program was entirely useless."[13] To "Considerações sobre a arte contemporânea" [Considerations on Contemporary Art], from 1952, Costa adds one word only: "Perfect."[14]

In the third category, we may highlight Costa's amendment to a note from the editor concerning the authorship of the project for the campus of the University of Brazil in Rio de Janeiro (according to the note, the project developed by Costa's team had had "Le Corbusier as a consultant"). Costa's note ("On the contrary, this project ensued the rejection of Le Corbusier's project by the Faculty Senate. Our *parti* was opposite to Le Corbusier's. It was central and dense, rather than rarefied and peripheral. Le Corbusier had no participation.") attests that, thirty years later, the authorship of the projects developed in the wake of Le Corbusier's stay in Rio in 1936 (namely, MES and University of Brazil) remained a matter of honor for Costa. More to the point, what remained intact was the need to reiterate – for posterity – that the design of both these projects was *ours*, not *his*. Now, that the notion of project employed by Costa in this and other occasions has hardly been the object of critical analysis by researchers only attests the authority of Costa's statements. Such authority persists. After all, even today there remain a consensus among Brazilian scholars that the design of MES was due to the Brazilian team; that Le Corbusier's contribution was restricted[15] – as Costa insisted – to a preliminary sketch.[16] Surprisingly, it was Oscar Niemeyer who, most recently, drew attention to the discrepancy between Le Corbusier's design methods and the one employed by Costa's team. Indeed, and notwithstanding Niemeyer's typical effort to highlight his own personal role in the episode in question, his testimony highlights the fact that without getting acquainted with Le Corbusier's innovative concepts and methods, neither of these two projects would have become what they are; that MES, in particular, would most likely keep the aspect of a "mummy" – i.e. the scorning nickname Le Corbusier gave to it the moment he saw its original blueprints.[17]

In that same category of notes are the extensive comments appended to the biographical note organized by José Carlos Coutinho. Here the highlight is Costa's unbound commitment to elucidate the role he had played in the process of discharging Archimedes Memoria's design for the MES building (in the wake of the national competition) and inviting Le Corbusier to Brazil in 1936. According to Coutinho,

Lúcio Costa, along with Carlos Drummond de Andrade, Mário de Andrade, Rodrigo Mello Franco de Andrade and Manuel Bandeira, took the initiative to convince the minister Gustavo Capanema about the need to discharge the award-winning design, and the need to inviting Le Corbusier to work as a guide for the development of a new project, one consistent with the time and impact of the work.[18]

Costa's refutation is peremptory: "Not true. I was asked to design a new building without having interfered in any way in this decision. The invitation to Le Corbusier came much later."[19] What is at stake for Costa is not – as it may seem at first glance – the need to downplay his own role in the episode of the invitation of the French architect, but rather to make clear that he had not took part in the shelving of Memoria's project. The fact that Costa had sent to Capanema an alternative project for the MES building a few weeks prior to the official announcement of the competition cancelation (Costa's letter dates from January 8, 1936, while Capanema's memo to Getúlio Vargas is from February 11th; the episode was only reported by the press at the beginning of March of the same year)[20] suggests, however, that Costa's role may have been less republican, so to speak, as he wants us to believe. In this case, as it becomes clear,

THE MARGINAL COMMENTS ARE AIMED AT CORROBORATING TWO OF THE MOST POPULAR TRAITS OF COSTA'S PERSONALITY, NAMELY RECTITUDE AND GENEROSITY.

Still in the third category is the rectification in the dating of "Razões da nova arquitetura" – a text regarded by many scholars as the conceptual touchstone of Brazilian modern architecture. About the context in which this text (published in January of 1936) was written, some confusion persists. In the autobiographical note Costa published in the book *Depoimento de uma geração*, also edited by Alberto Xavier and published in 1987, Costa wrote: "In 1935, I was a professor at Anísio Teixeira's University of the Federal District ("Razões da nova arquitetura")"[21] – implying, therefore, that the text had been written in this specific context. The information is corroborated by *Registro de uma vivência*, in which Costa refers to the text as the "program for a course at the Art Institute directed by Celso Kelly in the old University of the Federal District, founded by Anísio Teixeira with help from Mário de Andrade, Gilberto Freyre, Prudente de Morais Neto, Sérgio Buarque de Holanda, Portinari and Celso Antonio, among others."[22] The correction in this dating ("1933-5", instead of "1930")[23] is suggestive: Accurate or not (to my knowledge, there are no available documental sources to corroborate it), the note suggest at any rate that, from the perspective of the Costa of 1966, this pivotal text had been written, or rather nursed, during the extensive and fertile years of *chômage* (1932-35) – i.e., the years in which, as acknowledged in a letter to Le Corbusier, Costa committed himself to giving a "full circle" around the "clear block" of "imposing grandeur," – i.e. Le Corbusier's *oeuvre*.[24] The confrontation between "Razões" and the ideas of the first Le Corbusier seem to confirm Costa's allegation.

ELOQUENT SILENCES

But even more significant than Costas amendments are his eloquent silences, that is to say his muteness before texts about which one would expect at least some amount of clarification and/or revision.

Two of these silences are particularly suggestive. The first one refers to Costa's reply from 1948 to the public admonition made that same year by the journalist Geraldo Ferraz (who accused Costa of having overlooked the role palyed by Gregori Warchavchik to the renewal of Brazilian architecture). Costa's response was extremely harsh – not just with Ferraz but specially with Warchavchik:

What is at stake and sharpens the curiosity of architects and critics of European and American art is not exactly to know when or how or by whom the new architectural concept was brought to our country, but rather why, while almost everywhere the new architecture remained more or less limited to routine

---

formulas, it should have broken out here, roughly twelve years after being tried for the first time without major consequences, with such grace and self-confidence, with such peculiar character and so unusual and disconcerting a vigor. That is the question that matters and to whose clarification the pioneering work of our dear Gregorio and the peculiar personality of Flávio [Carvalho] cannot in any way help, because what took place here would have occurred, without even a single line of difference – even if the first had done his work elsewhere, and the second rested in exile, since he was a child, in Paris or Passárgada.[25]

If the reply from 1948 was tough, the silence of 1966 suggested that, nearly twenty years after, there was nothing to add to that unequivocal – and somewhat controversial – interpretation. And this despite the melancholic and unrelenting marginalization process into which "our dear Gregório" was embroiled. As Costa's silence makes clear, such marginalization was largely due to the force of his own interpretations.[26]

The second silence refers to the text "Oportunidade perdida" – that is, Costa's reply to the harsh critique that the Swiss architect and artist Max Bill made in 1953 to Brazilian contemporary architecture. Claiming to know "almost everything so far published abroad on Brazilian architecture," Bill had been in fact adamant: "modern Brazilian architecture suffers a little from that love to the useless, to the plainly decorative."[27] Once again, Costa's counterattack was harsh, almost coarse; more than refuting the ideas, he aimed at disqualifying the critic, who according to Costa "is not, strictly speaking, neither an architect nor a painter or a sculptor, but fundamentally an eyeliner of forms (*designer*)." Incidentally, Costa argued, if Brazilian architecture denoted certain *baroquism*, it was because, in his words, "we do not descend from watchmakers but from builders of baroque churches." The fact that after more than ten years, there was nothing to be added to the sheer devaluation of the notion of design, suggests that either a) Costa's disregard for the constructivism/Bauhausian branch of the modern movement (according to which, as is known, the distinction between the domains of industrial design and of architecture is problematic)[28] remained unaltered; or b) Costa kept believing that, in the specific case of Brazil, for various reasons (the main one, the paucity of Brazil's industrialization), the implementation of modern architecture should *still* rely on an alternative model, namely Corbusian technical formalism.[29]

ABOUT SOME EDITORIAL CRITERIA

That said, a number of editorial choices in the present edition seem questionable to me. The first one is the use of the same color (red earth) for both the book's original drawings and Costa's marginal notes – a choice that can easily confuse the unsuspecting reader. The same can be said of the set of updates and corrections (spelling, dating etc.) made to the original version: In the case of a facsimile edition, wouldn't it be wiser, for example, to keep the original version untouched, and complement it with endnotes?

Equally questionable – again, in terms of an edition that presents itself as a facsimile one – was the replacement of a number of drawings. It is not clear, for example, why drawings that in the original edition illustrated the text "Considerações sobre a arte contemporânea" should have been replaced by alternative ones. The question arises: Was there something wrong with the drawings published in the original edition? If not, what would justify their replacement? – the fact that Costa had published them in *Registro de uma vivência*? The caveat in the foreword to the present edition is not entirely clarifying:

With regard to spelling, dates, places, names, etc., these have
now been corrected in the text, while the observations of Lúcio

Costa on his drawings – sometimes missing in the original edition,

sometimes published as new versions – were replaced whenever

possible, as is the case of graphics on pages 206, 207 and 209.[30]

Now, does this mean that occasional additions and/or replacement of drawing implied the suppression of notes whereby Costa suggested these additions and/or replacements? And even if this has not occurred, which was the criteria employed in choosing what was and what was not *possible* to correct[31] – the acknowledgment, on the part of Xavier, of a mistake made back in 1962?, the vehemence of some of Costa's complaints?

That said, the republication of *Lúcio Costa: sobre arquitetura* – whose original version, long unavailable, had become a collector's item – is a great contribution (from the part of Alberto Xavier, to whose action scholars in Brazilian architecture are greatly indebted) to 20th century Brazilian intellectual history. For the contemporary reader, it offers a rare opportunity to have access to the original versions of Lúcio Costa's extraordinary writings. If there is something to regret, in this case, it is the fact that the reprint did not occur sooner, as Xavier had long planned. In a letter to him, dated October 13, 1971, Costa made clear, however, what he thought about Xavier's plans:

Dear Alberto Xavier, I do not understand your initiative, for it makes no sense, when the preparation of the definitive book about me is nearly finished, to harm it with the reprint of the publication made by CEUA without my consent. I assumed that after all conversations it was already clear in your spirit that this book by UnB – where my thinking would be coherently translated – would be the final word.[32]

Forty-five years after the original publication of *Lúcio Costa: sobre arquitetura*, it is once again time to go after the words of our master – that is to say, Lúcio Costa.[33]

NOTES

EN. This article is a review of the book *Lúcio Costa: sobre arquitetura*, written by Lúcio Costa. Article previously published at: Otavio Leonidio, "Em busca da palavra do mestre," *Novos Estudos Cebrap* 79, November 2007, 239-249.

1. Alberto Xavier, "Nota informativa," in Lúcio Costa, *Lúcio Costa: sobre arquitetura*, ed. Aberto Xavier (Porto Alegre: Ceua/UFRGS, 1962), 8.

2. Alberto Xavier, "Depoimento," in *Um modo de ser moderno: Lúcio Costa e a crítica contemporânea*, ed. Roberto Conduru, Ana Luiza Nobre, João Kamita and Otavio Leonidio (São Paulo: Cosac Naify, 2004), 311. Free translation.

3. Ibid.

4. Otília Arantes, "Resumo de Lúcio Costa," *Folha de S. Paulo*, February 24, 2006, 6-11; Carlos Alberto Ferreira Martins, "Arquitetura e Estado no Brasil. Elementos para uma análise da constituição do discurso moderno no Brasil. A obra de Lúcio Costa 1924-52" (master's thesis, FFLCH-USP, 1988).

5. In fact, this characteristic transform in puzzles the work of compilation of Lúcio Costa's articles – work that until these days remains unfinished.

6. I would point out, among others, the works – by definition, critics – of Luís Espallargas Gimenez, Carlos Alberto Ferreira Martins and Otília Beatriz Fiori Arantes.

7. Abilio Guerra, "Lúcio Costa: modernidade e tradição. Montagem discursiva da arquitetura moderna brasileira" (PhD diss., IFCH Unicamp, 2002).

8. In his foreword, Alberto Xavier says that of Lúcio Costa's published works, "in this book, only two articles were not included, both already well known: 'Arquitetura dos jesuítas no Brasil' and the preface of 'Antônio Francisco Lisboa'". Alberto Xavier, "Nota informativa," in Costa, *Lúcio Costa*, 10. Free translation.

9. Besides a small declaration made by Costa in 1931 and published in ENBA's annals.

10. Aleijadinho is the nickname of Antonio Francisco Lisboa, designer of baroque religious architecture and sculpture in 18th century Minas Gerais.

11. Alberto Xavier, "Impertinência necessária," in Costa, *Lúcio Costa*, XVII.

---

12. TN: As the campus of the Federal University in Rio is called in Brazil

13. Ibid., 160. Free translation.

14. Ibid., 229.

15. Ibid., 67.

16. Otavio Leonidio, "Carradas de razão: Lúcio Costa e a arquitetura moderna brasileira (1924-1951)" (PhD diss., PUC-Rio, 2005), 171-172.

17. Niemeyer's statement was published in *O risco. Lúcio Costa e a utopia moderna*, ed. Guilherme Wisnik (Rio de Janeiro: Bang Bang Filmes, 2003), 110-120.

18. Costa, *Lúcio Costa*, 352. Free translation.

19. Ibid.

20. Maurício Lissovsky and Paulo Sérgio M. Sá. *Colunas da educação: a construção do Ministério da Educação e Saúde* (Rio de Janeiro: IPHAN, 1996), 25-29.

21. Lúcio Costa, "Autobiografia [2/9/1987, atribuída]," in *Depoimento de uma geração*, ed. Alberto Xavier (São Paulo: Pini/Asbea/Fundação Vilanova Artigas, 1987), 331-334. Free translation.

22. Lúcio Costa, *Lúcio Costa: registro de uma vivência* (São Paulo: Empresa das Artes, 1995), 108, header.

23. Notice that, both in the original and in the recent edition, it was chosen to date the articles *whenever possible* because the date of its elaboration, and not of its publication.

24. Lúcio Costa, "Carta a Le Corbusier, 26/6/1936," quoted in Cecilia

Rodrigues dos Santos, Margareth da Silva Pereira, Vasco Caldeiras da Silva and Romão Veriano da Silva Pereira, *Le Corbusier e o Brasil* (São Paulo: Tassela/Projeto, 1987), 141-142.

25. Lúcio Costa, "Carta depoimento," *O Jornal*, March 14, 1948. Free translation.

26. Carlos Martins, "Gregori Warchavchik: combates pelo futuro," in Gregori Warchavchik, *Arquitetura do século XX e outros escritos*, ed. Carlos A. F. Martins (São Paulo: Cosac Naify, 2006).

27. Max Bill, "Max Bill critica a nossa moderna arquitetura," *Manchete* 60, June 13, 1953, 38-39, quoted in *Arte concreta paulista: documentos*, ed. João Bandeira (São Paulo: Cosac Naify, 2002), 32-33. Free translation.

28. This theme is been pioneered discussed by Ana Luiza Nobre in her PhD research, developed at Post Graduate Program in Social History of Culture at PUC-Rio.

29. Giulio Carlo Argan, "Arquitetura moderna no Brasil," *Comunità* 24, 1954, 48-52, quoted in *Depoimento de uma geração*, 174.

30. Costa, *Sobre arquitetura*, XVII. Highlights of the author. Free translation.

31. There are comments in which Costa protests against the absence of illustrations and, even then, the editor didn't answered the request.

32. Lúcio Costa, "Carta a Alberto Xavier," *October* 13, 1971. Free translation.

33. Reproduced (facsimile) at Leonidio, "Carradas de razão," 367.

CONCRETISM, NEO-CONCRETISM AND THE CONTEMPORARY

TRANSLATED BY GABRIEL POMERANCBLUM

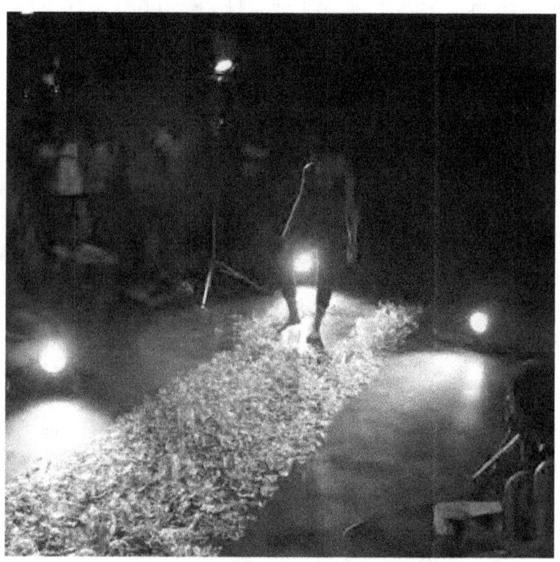

Symbebekos, Juliana Notari. MAM, Rio de Janeiro RJ, March 2011.
Photo Otavio Leonidio

Seeing Mondrian as a destroyer of the surface, the plan, and the
line is pointless unless we focus on the new space built up by
this destruction.

Ferreira Gullar, *Manifesto neo-concreto*, 1959. Free translate.

How contemporary is contemporary art in Brazil?

The question seems out of place and order, extraneous to
the triumphalist mood that characterizes the ongoing – and
much-hailed – international recognition of Brazil's contemporary
art, in particular its founding fathers and mothers, namely Hélio
Oiticica and Lygia Clark. In what follows, I intend to show that the
question is not only pertinent but also necessary.

In order to do that, I will address one specific work – the
performance *Symbebekos*, enacted in March 2011 by Juliana
Notari in the open ground floor of the Museum of Modern Art
in Rio de Janeiro – MAM. And as a critical framework, I will
adopt two dominant interpretations of contemporary art in
Brazil, namely: a) the rise of concretism in the early 1950s in
São Paulo marks the depletion of the *modernist* cycle in Brazil's
visual arts (which, in the specific case of Brazil, is marked by a
strong sense of nationalism, one that is hardly consistent with
some of the core values of modern art, namely its characteristic universalism) and ushers in the modern cycle; and b) the

advent of neo-concretism in Rio de Janeiro in the end of that same decade constitutes an overcoming of concretism – more pointedly, of its radical rationalism, in favor of more phenomenological approach to art making.

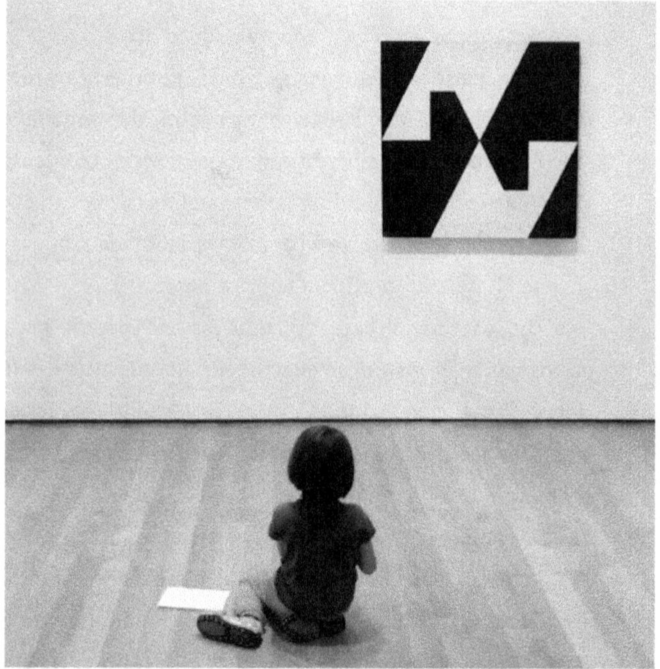

Plans in Modulated Surface 4, Lygia Clark, 1957. MoMA, New York NY, 2010. Photo Otavio Leonidio

Let us begin with the former – the oft-repeated interpretation according to which concretism marks the depletion of the modernist cycle in Brazil's visual arts, and ushers in the modern cycle. That thesis does not simply imply that the advent of concretism entails the end of the nationalist ideology inehrent in Brazil's modernist movement, that such ideology simply ceases to exist. Rather, it means that it is no longer recognized by cutting-edge artists and critics as the flagship of the avant-garde.

In practice, the advent of concretism marks the end of the rule of so called *brasilidade modernista* (literally, modernist brazilness), a period in which each and every avant-garde artwork in Brazil (following the agenda set up in the mid-1920s in São Paulo by modernism's chief theorists, the writers Mário de Andrade and Oswald de Andrade) was deemed to embody and convey the true spirit, the autentic character, the countenance of the Brazilian culture.[1]

The advent and rise to prominence of one such rigorous nationalist agenda would raise significant constraints to the renewal of Brazilian art. Let me quote in this respect two important interpreters of Brazil's modernist movement – Carlos Zílio and Ronaldo Brito. What did they say? In *A querela do Brasil*, Zílio stressed the way in which Brazil's modernist/nationalist ideology would impose unsurmountable limits to the renovation of visual arts in Brazil:

---

after an early, disoriented spell of destruction of academicism, the modernists of the [1922] Week offer a project for Brazilian culture. While denying rhetorical nationalism, they aspire to globalize the Brazilian imaginary, creating unity by incorporating formative cultural sources, contributions from the popular realm, and the contemporaneity of art from developed industrial societies. In art, the works of Tarsila [do Amaral] would be the most accomplished example of that recipe for an anthropophagical soup.[2]

The main consequence of such quest for unity – that is to say, in practice, the urge to reconcile factors that looked hardly compatible, namely, on the one hand, Brazil's popular cultural heritage, and on the other, the tenets of the European avant-garde, in particular futurism and cubism – was, in Zilio's words, painting becoming "narrative and traditional, with a modern veneer."[3] Not surprisingly, Zílio asserts, Brazil's modernism would connect itself to the least challenging of all the available trends in the international scenario:

In seeking contemporaneity, [Brazil's] modernism connected with currents that no longer represented the more renewal-oriented movements. In being influenced by second-tier

CONCRETISM, NEO-CONCRETISM

AND THE CONTEMPORARY

School of Paris artists, or in reiterating the more conventional aspects of Matisse and Picasso – with the partial exception of Tarsila regarding Léger –, the Brazilian movement displayed its constructive shortcomings. Modernism did not possess the structural conditions to grasp the constructive movements, dadaism, and surrealism, except for its more apparent procedures.[4]

Ronaldo Brito, in the essay "A Semana de 22: o trauma do moderno" is even more emphatic. I say more emphatic because unlike Zílio, Brito does not concede to the modernists of the 1920s the merit of having challenged what Zílio dubs "the dominant ideology." Here is Brito's take on the question of brazilness:

Much more of a sentiment than it is a concept, almost a phantasmal over-determination, [the agenda of *brazilness* all but imposed on our artists what European modernity had disavowed since Manet – the primacy of the theme, the subordination of painting to the subject. Reencountering, embracing, or even projecting Brazil of necessity entailed giving it a face, a countenance. For to descend to the deepest layers of visuality, to explore its most abstract articulations, would be an

---

impossibility while bound by the commitments of one particular figuration. And all the more so with the goal of envisioning and building a Brazilian visual identity using artistic raw materials completely unlike those that were being received from Europe. No wonder the results were somewhat inadequate. The ensuing relationship between Portinari and his phantom, Picasso, is very enlightening in that respect.[5]

Just like Zílio, Brito stresses how the nationalist agenda would entailed in practice an awkward compromise between the realms of the literary and the visual:

What is seldom, if ever, discussed, is the literary character of the ideology of Brazilianness. The evident fact that it is word, first and foremost, and therefore it infuses contents into the work of the painters and sculptors from the outside in. Thus, despite of our advances, we remained bound to cultural tradition of Portugal: the word would altogether control the eye, which had no power of signification in and of itself... the currency and urgency of the theme of Brazilianness in the fine arts, and the resulting subordination of the eye to a merely illustrative intelligence, is inseparable from the Portuguese heritage of the totalitarianism of the word. cubism, fauvism, suprematism, neo-plasticism are exclusively or predominantly visual instances of modernism. The occasional Brazilian translation, however, would always happen through the filter of Brazilianness. The fixation of Brazilian fine arts enunciations, for the most part amenable to verbalization, seemed to be a structural need of our modernism... This particular datum regarding our modernism – its achievement in the face of Europeanizing academicism – was nevertheless, to an extent, at odds with modernity itself.[6]

In order to illustrate the dominance of this line of interpretation, let me quote another renowned Brazilian critic, Paulo Sérgio Duarte. According to him,

[o]ur modernism is shy and bashful, like one who leaves the slave farm for the city and tries not to show – rightly so, by the way – their recent enslaved, ignorant past. Tarsila's brilliant pictures, which are part of our art history, have nothing anthropophagic about them, except for the title of one of them. At no time does form devour the *foreign*. The assimilation of cubist and post-cubist lessons, already underway during the 1920s, encountered a conciliatory adaptation in the Brazilian realm.[7]

According to these interpretations, in sum, what concretism, and later neo-concretism, had accomplished was putting an end to a shy and bashful, fledgling and conciliatory form of modernism – one that, on all accounts, could never be considered properly modern. Hence the idea – sumarized once again by Brito – that only after the downfall of the modernist cicle, would Brazilian art enter the space of modernity:

In Brazil... modern art, in its fundamental concepts, would not be truly comprehended and practiced until the *constructivist avant-garde* came about. Tarsila, Di Cavalcanti, Guignard, Portinari and others made the passage and played a role more or less similar to that of the groups that preceded the emergence of suprematism and constructivism in Russia... The 50s were the decade in which the Brazilian art set began to deal with the concepts of modern art and the implications thereof... And the contact with those concepts is what gave rise to the concrete and neo-concrete discourses, with the overt intention of carrying them on... It was about carrying on with the work of Maliêvitch and Mondrian, and of Max Bill and the Swiss concretists on a closer front. The prize that the 1951 São Paulo Art Biennial awarded Bill's *Unit of three equal volumes* was a symptom of local enthusiasm about the

CONCRETISM, NEO-CONCRETISM

AND THE CONTEMPORARY

rationalistic postulates of concrete art. That enthusiasm…

triggered an unequivocal geometric trend, and the

constructivist concepts that that trend implied.[8]

Again, Brito is not alone in stressing the role that constructivist avant-gardes (namely De Stijl and Russion constructivism) had played in Brazil's quest for *true* modernity. As a case in point, I quote the English critic and curator Guy Brett, one of the pioneers in promoting neo-concretism outside Brazil. In his words

The full impact of those ideas [20th century avant-garde

ideas] in Brazil coincides with the moment, shortly after

the war, that Lygia [Clark] and Brazil's other great innovator,

Hélio Oiticica, began to work. Both artists regarded Mondrian

and Malevich as their mentors. They were drawn to those

artists as ones who, so they believed, had strayed the most

decisively from pictorial representation tools – illusionism,

depth, perspective – that were inherited from Renaissance…

However, as one can see in their writings and statements,

Lygia and Hélio took the achievements of the abstract

pioneers not only as a formal and conceptual trend, but also

phenomenologically: that the new space can somehow be

sensually *experienced*… It's as if Mondrian had set the stage for Lygia Clark's journey beyond the optical.[9]

As is clear, Brett emphasizes not so much the first as what I referred to in the outset as the second dominant interpretation of Brazil's contemporary art, namely that the advent of neo-concretism in Rio implies the overcoming of concretism's rationalist orthodoxy, in favor of a more phenomenological approach to art making.

In order to illustrate the power of this reading I could once again refer to Ronaldo Brito's interpretation – namely, to the set of oppositions he establishes between, on the one hand, the concretist orthodoxy (with its rationalistic reductionism), and on the other hand, the libidinal, experiential, emotional, erotic, phenomenological, and expressive aspects of neo-concretism.[10] Instead, I shall resort to a historical document – the "Manifesto neoconcreto," written and published in 1959 by the poet Ferreira Gullar, and undersigned by artists Amílcar de Castro, Franz Weissmanm, Lygia Clark, Lygia Pape, Reynaldo Jardim, and Theon Spanúdis, besides Gullar himself. The rejection of concretism's inflexible rationalism comes in the opening lines of the text:

The term neo-concrete is a stand taken regarding non-figurative *geometric* art (neo-plasticism, constructivism, suprematism, the Ulm School), and particularly regarding concrete art driven to a dangerous rationalist exacerbation.

Gullar goes on:

Malevich, having recognized the primacy of *pure sensibility in art*, spared his theoretical definitions of the limitations of rationalism and mechanicism, endowing his paintings with a transcendent dimension that ensures their remarkable currency until this day... Rationalism robs art of all autonomy, replacing the nontransferable qualities of the work of art with notions from scientific objectivity: thus, the concepts of form, space, time, structure – which in the language of the arts are tied with an existential, emotional, affective signification – become confused with the theoretical application that science gives them.[11]

As is clear, more than a statement in support of neo-concretism, Gullar's manifesto is an outcry against concretism. That is, more than a praise of neo-concrete's sensibility, emotion and affectivity, the text is an admonition of concretism's rationalism, scientism, and objectivity. And according to

Gullar, there were very good reasons for one such reproach; after all, from a phenomenological perspective, concretism had simply ignored the evidence that there is no such thing as an un-sensitive form of art; that resensitizing concretism (as Rio's artists were set to do) didn't simply mean updating or improving an outmoded artistic movement; ultimately, it meant transforming non-art into art.

Written and published in 1959, the "Manifesto neo-concreto" does not address the core issue of the present essay, namely the passage from the modern condition to a contemporary one. The rise of "the contemporary" as a central category of both art history and art criticism dates from more recent years, and follows the exhaustion of the category postmodern, and even more so of postmodernism, both of which being increasingly regarded as unfit to a contemporary – i.e. essentially non-modern – temporal experience (the primary problem being, in both cases, the use of the prefix *post*, that is a typically historicist semantic device).[12] Which doesn't mean that the question regarding the contemporaneity of neo-concretism was not central to the signatories of the "Manifesto." It was. Yet as far as Gullar and his comrades were concerned, asserting the contemporaneity of neo-concretism did not require relinquishing the constructivist tradition. On the contrary, it meant restating what they believed had been misinterpreted and corrupted by their peers in Sao Paulo, who in their determination to "see man as a machine among machines," had completely missed the lessons of Malevich and Mondrian. That this was indeed the notion of the contemporary around which neo-concretism had been built is confirmed by the critic Mário Pedrosa, who in 1967 defiantly asked:

And, above all, who would deny, today, the remarkable contemporaneity of the Rio neo-concrete movement for the utterly audacious plastic experiments of the utmost *avant-garde*?[13]

As is often is the case, it fell to historiography, and not to artists themselves, the task of defining neo-concretism as the gateway to the contemporary – thus defined not merely as another stage in Brazil's constructive epopee, but instead as a rupture with the artistic trends that preceded it. Even more than the two interpretations aforementioned, this thesis (i.e. the idea that neo-concretism amounts to a historical rupture with the movements that preceded it and, as such, constitutes a passage-way to the contemporary) is what I would like to discuss henceforth.

Once again, I shall quote Ronaldo Brito, in particular his allegation that neo-concretism "broke the sequence of constructive development" and "laid the groundwork for contemporary art in Brazil."[14] Underpinning Brito's reading is the idea that, ultimately, the cultural meaning of neo-concretism dwells in its refusal to carry on with "a project that was to an extent messianic, which involved a sequence of efforts to overcome underdevelopment."[15] That is, according to Brito's reading the contemporaneity of neo-concretism lays not so much, or at least not exclusively, in its option for a more phenomenological approach to art making, but mostly in its aptitude to lay bare and confront the contradictions inherent in Brazil's constructivist project – mainly due to the unreserved faith it kept in Brazil's *developmentalist* ideology of the 1950s, with its virulent, unlimited strive for industrialization, productivity, and rationalization of local reality.

What is of particular interest in Brito's characterization, therefore, is not so much the assertion of neo-concretism as an authentic version of contemporary aesthetics, but the bonds his readings establishes between the notion of the contemporary and dominant political ideologies, in this case represented by the ideology of developmentalism. For Brito, indeed, being contemporary in Brazil required more than simply taking part in the

CONCRETISM, NEO-CONCRETISM

AND THE CONTEMPORARY

aesthetic renewal of art, but above all else affirming art's autonomy *vis-à-vis* the status quo. (Implicit in this reading, therefore, is the idea that if concretism succeeded in ridding Brazilian art of nationalisti ideologies, it failed to do the same in regard to the developmentalist ideology: In any event, art remained instrumental, that is to say at the service of non-artistic agendas.)

From Brett's perspective (i.e., from the standpoint of a detached member of the international avant-garde establishment), on the other hand, the contemporaneity of neo-concretism could not be dissociated from the one inherent in the most challenging art of the 1960s and 70s – namely minimalism and post-minimalism. In his words,

Lygia [Clark]'s renewal of the *cannibalistic* concept worked in

many extremely important and subtle ways to set her work

apart from that of many of her visual art contemporaries in

Europe and North America, with whom she shared a few formal

commonalities. Her proposal of the object's *incorporation* by

the spectator gave her a radically different conceptual stance

from both the avant-garde sculpture that emerged in the 60s

and the body art that came later, even though Lygia can be

considered an innovator in purely sculptural terms, just as she

can be considered a pioneer of the *return to the body*, often described as one of most prominent features of recent art. Lygia Clark's rubber *Obra mole* predated such works as Morris' floppy felt sculptures and Richard Serra's rubber *Rosa Esman's Piece* by several years (a fact unknown to European and American art history)... Her *Máscaras Abismo* have parallels on a formal level to Hesse's softly-hanging netted weights, such as Hesse's *Untitled sculpture* of 1966, but the differences are obvious. Morris, Serra and Hesse's pieces are objects for the sight. Lygia Clark's have neither existence nor meaning without the support and manipulation of the human being.[16]

Even more than its ambivalences (according to Brett, Brazilian art is both divergent from and aligned with contemporary European and North American art) what springs to attention in Brett's interpretation is the way he regards the work of Lygia Clark, which he sees as anticipatory *vis-à-vis* the works of leading American artists of the 1960s and 70s. And if Brett does not insist much on the thesis of anticipation, pure and simple, it is because, to his eyes, Clark's work is... *far more contemporary than the work of her American peers* (whose "objects for the sight," according to Brett, were meant for aesthetic contemplation only, while the works by Brazilian artists had "neither existence nor meaning without the support and manipulation of the human being").

I am ready to talk about *Symbebekos* now.

As an artistic manifestation, *Symbebekos* clearly falls in the category performance – which, in the wake of the self-purging agenda set by minimalist artists in the early 1960s, rose to prominence toward the end of that same decade as a quintessential practice of contemporary aesthetics. More pointedly, *Symbebekos* fits into one of the most typical modalities of performance art – one whereby the performer strictly abides by a task or script she previously set to herself. On all accounts, *Symbebekos* belongs in the domain of the contemporary.

In the case of *Symbebekos*, however, and unlike the proverbially boring performances by a Bruce Nauman, for example (have in mind *Walking in an Exaggerated Manner around the Perimeter of a Square*, from 1967-68), the task at hand presents itself from the outset as particularly arduous and risky: The performer must tread a trail littered with hundreds, thousands of glass shards.[17] The fact that Juliana Notari was assigned to close, at seven-thirty in the evening, an event that had begun at two in the afternoon that day led to a colective escalating expectation from the part of the audience, as in between performances attendants unavoidably came across that roped-off carpet of glass shards.

Notari's performance began roughly at the designated time, and within some 20 minutes she had accomplished her task quite satisfactorily: With much skill, she managed to tread the trail of glass shards she herself had laid, leaving behind her a subtle yet perceivable trail of blood.

But that is merely the contemporary dimension (or the contemporary account) of *Symbebekos*.

FOR A NUMBER OF PARTICULARITIES IN NOTARI'S ACTION SUGGEST THAT, WHILE THE ARTIST HAD ONE FOOT FIRMLY PLANTED ON THE SPACE OF THE CONTEMPORARY, THE OTHER TROD UPON – AND ALSO UNDERNEATH – THE SPACE OF MODERNITY.

Proof of that is the submission to the space and the temporality of the Museum of Modern Art. Indeed, out of all possible arrangements, Juliana Notari performed her walk along glass shards not only in the open ground floor of the building designed in the 1950s by Brazilian architect Affonso E. Reidy, but specifically along its longitudinal central axis. In doing so, albeit in an unusual way, she unequivocally reiterated not just the axis itself, but the overall spatial logic defined by Reidy's design – namely, the linear sequence of monumental concrete porticoes that expand and proliferate in a catenated march along that same axis.

It doesn't seem fortuitous, on that account, that just as the trail of glass reproduced this virtual longitudinal axis, the direction followed by Notari's walk also emulated the temporal development of the building, which, starting with the construction of the school block in 1958, would only be achieved roughly a decade later, with the construction of the main exhibition block.

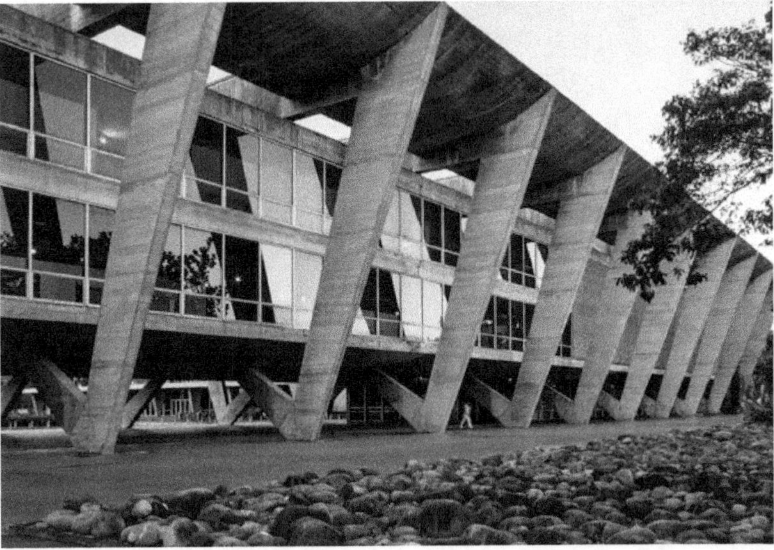

Museum of Modern Art, Rio de Janeiro RJ. Affonso Eduardo Reidy, 1953. Photo Nelson Kon

---

Ultimately, therefore, and notwithstanding the contemporary profile of the action, *Symbebekos* both emulates and reinstates the spatiality of Reidy's building. In doing so, thoughtfully or not, the action partook in the overall ideology underlying the construction of this building – an ideology whose great epigone on the domain of architecture is Reidy, and whose greatest architectural achievement is indeed MAM.

It's not surprising that *Symbebekos* brings to mind one specific historic character: Max Bill – not so much the fierce critic of Brazilian modern architecture,[18] but Bill the great admirer of Affonso Eduardo Reidy, i.e. the designer of the Pedregulho residential compound, which Bill saw as the greatest achievement of modern architecture in Brazil. In an interview published on a 1953 MAM bulletin, Bill touted his admiration for Reidy:

From an urbanistic standpoint, Brazilian architecture is catastrophic. And this cannot be remedied by any modern architectural work, however high its quality, unless it has been established within a social plan. But I have seen the Pedregulho residential compound and I have a flicker of hope. It is one of the most humane and advanced accomplishments I have had the chance to see so far. You can take pride in this achievement here, in Rio, and I must congratulate a community that has workers who are fighting for the future and the present. Pedregulho is an urbanistic, architectural and social triumph.[19]

Bill's interview was published a few years prior to the opening of MAM. I don't know whether or not he visited the Museum after the work's completion. I wonder in any event what would have crossed his mind in seeing the works on show during the golden (and now mythic) days of neo-concretism – all the sensuous, emotional, libidinal objects and non-objects that would make the fame of Brazilian contemporary art. My guess is that he would have reacted with indifference: In the face of evidence that a Brazilian alternative to the European constructivist project (of which Bill had been one the most ardent enthusiasts)[20] was doomed to failure; that it could never live up to the barbarism and irrationality of Brazil's most prominent and influential architect, Oscar Niemeyer (according to whom, one should not forget, "Bauhaus was shit").

Yet, I don't think Bill would be indifferent to *Symbebekos* and its awkward submission to the space of Reidy's building. Perhaps he would have judged that right there, before his eyes, however unlikely, was the expression of what was left, glass shards and blood trails included, of an ideology which, from the Deutscher

Werkbund to the Bauhaus, and from this one to Ulm, had envisioned the aesthetization/rationalization of modern life – the ideology that, transposed to Brazil, had birthed Pampulha and Brasília, Pedregulho and *Symbebekos*; the project that, like it or not, and notwithstanding neo-concretism's phenomenological argument, pervades Lygia Clark's rigorous *Bichos* (whose style, in Donald Judd's eyes, was nothing more than "ordinary capable constructivism."),[21] Hélio Oiticica's neo-neoplastic sub-architecture (whoever has been to Inhotim and penetrated *Magic Square #5* should know what I mean), the lyrical, scenographic, and rather easy constructivism of Lygia Pape's *Teteia*.

AM I DEMEANING THESE WORKS? NOT NECESSARILY. I AM SIMPLY UNDERSCORING THAT, LIKE IT OR NOT, THE CONSTRUCTIVIST IDEOLOGY INFORMS THEIR LIFEBLOOD.

More: That being subject, as they have been of late, to an icon-building process, these works have become exempted from critical reading, i.e. from analyses that while acknowledging their aesthetical quality and power do not resign the task of pinpointing their specificities, shortcomings and contradictions – and, even more so, the unusual conception of the contemporary these works seem to evoque. I am not properly referring to the fact that since they have been treated as a more or less cohesive, uniform block, not much is said of the less interesting part of that output; rather, I am thinking about the questions raised by the *more interesting and powerful work* produced by artists such as Clark, Oiticia and Pape.

Let me give an example. Although it is much discussed whether Lygia Clark's last works belong in the domain of art or rather to psychotherapy, little attention has been paid to the fact that the supposed conversion they promote from a "passive subject of contemplation" into an "active subject of participation"[22] as a rule kept Clark in the position (even physically so) of an active, purposeful agent – as opposed to the passive position her subjects occupy during her experiments. This aspect gains relevance if one considers, once again, some of the more paradigmatic performances of the 1960s and the 70s, in which artists oftentimes assume an essentially passive attitude, remaining quite often literally at the mercy of the other people's actions (consider, for instance, Yoko Ono's "Cut Piece" in which audience members cut the artist's clothes to pieces, as the artist remains motionless).[23]

Another issue I believe needs discussing concerns the legacy of these artists. I do not mean the fact that their output has remained under the strict control of their vigilant, and often-times seemingly opportunist, decendents – with the nefarious consequences that many of us are aware of.[24] I mean the fact that that output not only lends itself to but actually elicits the – not rarely regrettable – use that has been made of it lately. Indeed, the ease with which these artworks had been filling the space of

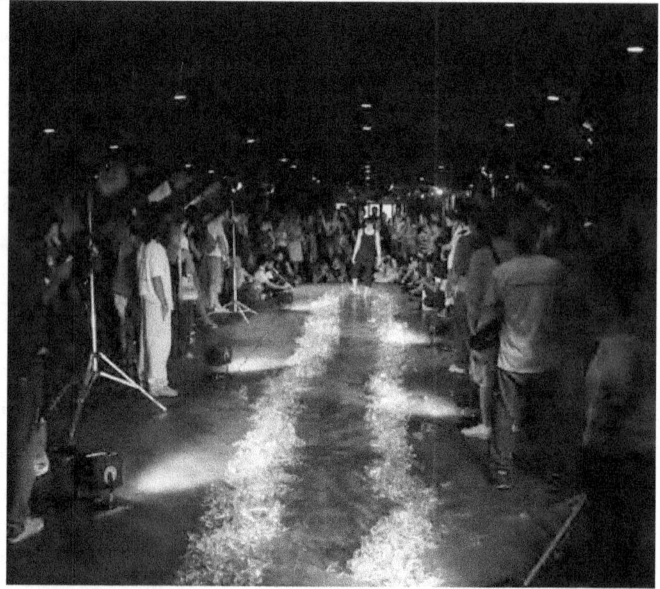

Symbebekos, Juliana Notari. MAM, Rio de Janeiro RJ, March 2011.
Photo Otavio Leonidio

CONCRETISM, NEO-CONCRETISM

AND THE CONTEMPORARY

trendy galleries, luxurious private collections, and spectacularized museums of modern and contemporary art – especially the top-tier ones, beginning with New York's MoMA and its Brazilian avatar, the MAM in Rio – jumps to attention. To argue that this phenomenon is unrelated to the concretist and neo-concretist ideologies sounds naïve to me; as far as I am concerned, there is something in these works that often puts them in a conformist, conservative cultural position. What gets conserved in this case seems clear to me – namely a nostalgic yearning for the modern condition – one without which, as one can see, Brazilian artists feel groundless.

And it is precisely because of its unrestrained, awkward attachment to the MAM's physical and institutional space, coupled with its undisguisable contemporary performativity, that *Symbebekos* proves so notably able to speak of Brazil's modern and contemporary experiences. For in this performance one can perceive both the expression of a painful quest (the one which, in fits and starts, for good or bad, led us from modernist brazilness to modernity, and from modernity to the contemporary) and the embodiment of Brazil's most recurrent dilemmas, including the unwillingness in letting go of a modernity which somehow both pulls us closer to and away from the space of the contemporary – at least from a contemporary understood as a rupture with the modern condition. More than a hybrid, *Symbebekos* seems like a contradiction in terms: On the one hand, it embodies the commitment to the deconstruction of the modernist being in the world; on the other, it enacts the unrelenting de-repression of Brazil's constructivist *pathos*, synthesized by neo-concretist postulate according to which any aesthetic destruction in Brazil would not be justified unless a construction ensued.

And so she goes, she runs, she seeks. What does she is seeks?[25] Bare feet, dressed in black, treading a beautiful, orderly – near-aseptic – road, walking in a straight line, along an architectural space that proved to be not as free as she had imagined, under the weight of the huge vaulted ceiling, echoing the rhythmic progression of those reinforced concrete porticoes, quiet and focused, hand in hand with a legion of ancestors, before the attentive, solidary eyes of the local avant-garde establishment, showing no sign of pain or fatigue, leaving behind her a trail of blood, she tries at all costs – *helás!* – to overcome modernity.

NOTES

AN. I am thankful to Luís Camillo Osório, Rodrigo Naves, Flávio Moura and Maria Palmeiro for their reading and comments.

EN. Article previously published at: Otavio Leonidio, "Caminhos comoventes: concretismo, neoconcretismo e arte contemporânea no Brasil."

CONCRETISM, NEO-CONCRETISM

AND THE CONTEMPORARY

Viso: Cadernos de Estética Aplicada 13, January/June 2013, 93-116.

1. Eduardo Jardim Moraes, *Limites do moderno. O pensamento estético de Mário de Andrade* (Rio de Janeiro: Relume Dumará, 1999).

2. Carlos Zilio, *A querela do Brasil. A questão da identidade da arte brasileira: a obra de Tarsila , Di Cavalcanti e Portinari/1922-1945* (Rio de Janeiro: FUNARTE, 1982), 113. Free translation.

3. Ibid., 114. Free translation.

4. Ibid., 116. Free translation.

5. Ronaldo Brito, "A Semana de 22. O trauma do moderno," in *Sete ensaios sobre o modernismo*, ed. Sérgio Tolipan, Silvano Santiago and José Miguel Wisnik (Rio de Janeiro: FUNARTE, 1983). Free translation.

6. Ibid. Free translation.

7. Paulo Sérgio Duarte, *Anos 60. Transformações da arte no Brasil* (Ponta Grossa: Campos Gerais Editora, 1998), 19. Free translation. The edition that I worked with bore the inscription "Special edition for my friends at Rede Globo." Wow!

8. Ronaldo Brito, *Neoconcretismo. Vértice e ruptura do projeto construtivo brasileiro* (São Paulo: Cosac Naify, 1999). 36-37. Free translation.

9. Guy Brett, "Lygia Clark: seis células," in *Lygia Clark*, Exhibition Catalogue [MAC, Marseille, 1998; Fundação Serralves, Porto, 1998; Palais des Beaux-Arts, Bruxelas, 1998; Paço Imperial, Rio de Janeiro, 1998-99] (Barcelona: Fundación Antoni Tàpies, 1997), 22-23. Free translation.

10. Brito, *Neoconcretismo*, passim.

11. Ferreira Gullar, "Manifesto neo-concreto," in *1ª Exposição Neocon-concreta*, Exhibition Catalogue (Rio de Janeiro: Museu de Arte Moderna do Rio de Janeiro, 1959). Free translation.

12. "every discourse on postmodernity is a contradictory one". Gianni Vattimo, *The End of Modernity* (Cambridge: Polity Press, 1988), 4.

13. Mário Pedrosa, "Um passeio pelas Caixas do passado [1967]," in Pedrosa, *Mundo*, 154. Free translation.

14. Brito, *Neoconcretismo*, 77 and 83. Free translation. I am thus deliberately disegarding the connotation Mário Pedrosa imparts to the notion of postmodern art. See Mário Pedrosa, "Crise do condicionamento artístico [1966]," in Pedrosa, *Mundo, homem, arte em crise* (São Paulo: Perspectiva, 2007), 92.

15. Ibid., 47. Free translation.

16. Brett, "Lygia Clark," 24. Free translation.

17. It is worth pointing out that an important precedent of Notari's performance is *Through the night softly* (1973), by Chris Burden.

18. Max Bill, "Max Bill critica a nossa moderna arquitetura," *Manchete* 60 (June 1953), quoted in *Arte concreta paulista: documentos*, ed. João Bandeira (São Paulo: Cosac Naify, 2002), 32-33.

19. Bill, "Visita ao Brasil do famoso escultor modernista," *Boletim do MAM* 9 (July 1953), quoted in *Arte concreta*, 30. Free translation.

20. See Max Bense, *Brasílianische Intelligenz. Eine Cartesianische Reflexion* (Wiesbaden: Limes Verlag, 1965); Sigfried Giedion, *A Decade of*

New Architecture (Zurich: Editions Girsberger, 1951).

21. Donald Judd, "In the Galleries," *Arts Magazine* 37, April 1963. Free translation.

22. Duarte, *Anos 60*, 60. Free translation.

23. Another example is the 1975 performance where Chris Burden puts his own survival in the audience's hands. www.rogerebert.com/interviews/chris-burden-my-god-are-they-going-to-leave-me-here-to-die.

24. "Manifesto em Defesa da Exibição Pública das Obras de Arte Brasileiras" ["Manifesto in Defense of the Public Exhibition of Brazilians Works of Art"]. www2.cultura.gov.br/site/wp-content/uploads/2009/08/manifesto.pdf.

25. "Ainsi il va, il court, il cherche. Que cherche-t-il?". Charles Baudelaire. *Écrits Sur L'art* (Paris: Le livre de Poche, 1992), 381. Originally published in *Le Figaro*, November 26 and 29 and December 3, 1863.

THE FOSTER-EISENMAN COMPLEX

TRANSLATED BY GABRIEL POMERANCBLUM

Architecture will always be presence. Whether architecture will continue to be legitimized by presence is what is really at issue.
Peter Eisenman, A Conversation with Peter Eisenman, 1997.

THE NEXUSES BETWEEN MODERN ART AND MODERN ARCHITECTURE ARE NOTORIOUS. IT WOULD BE LITERALLY IMPOSSIBLE TO ACCOUNT FOR THE ADVENT OF MODERN ARCHITECTURE WITHOUT MENTIONING ITS INDEBTEDNESS TO AVANT-GARDE ART, NAMELY CUBISM, DE STIJL, ITALIAN FUTURISM AND RUSSIAN CONSTRUCTIVISM. AS FOR THE NEXUSES between contemporary art and contemporary architecture, these are far more enigmatic: What the architectural métier refers to as minimalism has very little to do with what art critics usually define as the meaning of minimal art. This is not to say that the topic is entirely absent to the architectural dialogue: Every now and then discussions emerge – as for example when Otilia Arantes censured Josep Maria Montaner for his misuse of the category minimalist architecture – that is the architecture of Tadao Ando, Álvaro Siza and Paulo Mendes da Rocha, among others. What on the other hand seems to be in total absentia is the discussion about the nexuses between contemporary architecture and architectural criticism – as if the advent of so called postmodern condition did not affect architectural criticism, only architectural praxis.

In what follows I attempt to show how seemingly contemporary critical accounts such as Foster's may conceal an unwillingness to underscore, and occasionally open to scrutiny, the foundations of current critical discourse. And the reason for such unwillingness, I would like to claim, is the fact that quite often these foundations are imbedded in typically modernist worldviews – hence their inability to account for postmodern, meta-critical practices such as Eisenman's.

One sometimes becomes a critic or a historian for the same
reason that one often becomes an artist or an architect – out of
a discontent with the status quo and a desire for alternatives.
There are no alternatives without critique.[1]

This utterance, made by Hal Foster in the introduction of *The Art-Architecture Complex*, heralds much of what readers will find in the pages of this book – namely this: Like its closest predecessor (*Design and Crime*, from 2003), this book was conceived as an act of resistance. As such, it does not purport to be a comprehensive overview of art and architecture in the past few decades, but only a critical take on the status quo of contemporary art and architecture.

What Foster means here by "the contemporary" are two distinct but directly connected things: a) that which, in art and architecture, intends to go beyond modernism (i.e., according to Foster, that which corresponds to and/or expands upon the advent, in the 1960s, of minimalism and pop art, and which, in the case of architecture, primarily means the pivotal postmodernisms of Reyner Banham or Robert Venturi); and b) that which, within the broad spectrum of culture, reflects the advent of post-industrial capitalism.

On the architecture side, therefore, the highlight is on practices that best suit the overall logic and cunning of global capitalism. Understandably, the book pores over the work of leading exponents of today's star system – namely, Renzo Piano, Richard Rogers and Norman Foster; Zaha Hadid and Frank Gehry; Diller Scofidio + Renfro and Herzog & De Meuron.

To architects unfamiliar with leftwing critique, Foster's approach will seem both surprising and inordinate. The object of reverence and even worship in the métier of architecture, these characters are treated here as mere collaborators – as avatars of "global styles" whose role, in the end, is none other than to reiterate and even leverage the ploys of contemporary capitalism.

Obviously enough, *The Art-Architecture Complex* is not limited to a generic denunciation of the complicity purported to characterize these practices. As underscored by the book's title, the author intends to tackle something quite specific here – namely the nexus between architecture and art, or more to the point between architecture and avant-garde art.

Thus, the problem with the architecture of Zaha Hadid, for example, is not so much the option for emulating the aesthetics of the historical avant-gardes (something that Foster, a major champion of the notion of a neo-avant-garde, in principle would never reproach);[2] rather it is the fact that she turned her architecture into a neo-avant-gardist farce. More specifically, Hadid's crime was to convert the dynamic and material constructivism of Tátlin into a mere representation of the notions of dynamism and materiality. To Foster, this is indeed what happens with the buildings designed by Hadid: they "do not convey movement so much as they represent it – they are precisely frozen motion – and, more than a multiplicity of mobile views, they set up a sequence of stationary perspectives."[3]

Foster contrasts Hadid's fake neo-avant-gardism to the work of the New York firm Diller Scofidio + Renfro (DS+R). Unlike Hadid, DS+R allegedly made a lateral turn,[4] that is focused not on the recent past, but instead in what was being made on the visual arts since the 1960s, with an emphasis on minimalism and post-minimalism.

The choice was productive, Foster concedes. Nonetheless, the loose ends are many; the main one was having remained "in the ambiguous position of much postmodernist art – that it to say, in a deconstructive position that, as it spoke within the conventions and institutions that it sought to question, often shaded into complicity with them." More specifically, Foster claims, DS+R adopted an ambivalent stance regarding the "effects of new media and technologies on space and subjectivity" – which, in practice, turned their buildings into a "mediated blend of screen-space."

THE FOSTER-EISENMAN COMPLEX

In doing so, DS+R committed what Foster regards as a mortal sin, no less – namely not engaging "corporeal experience very deeply" thus contributing to the proliferation of "an already pervasive culture of special effects and faux phenomenologies."[5]

The censure evinces what, in Foster's view, is at stake when it comes to discussing the art-architecture complex as of today: The decline of experience – more specifically, of a phenomenological experience[6] diametrically opposed to the (seductive, spectacular, illusionistic) effects that characterize contemporary imagistic culture. To Foster's mind, this is indeed the distinguishing feature of current architecture: a shameless acceptance of the superficial and the imagetic, to the detriment of the spatial, the materic, and the tectonic. As evidence of this state of affairs, Foster cites the proliferation of so-called architectural skins – undeniably one of the distinguishing marks of architecture in the past few decades.

According to Foster, in making this choice for the superficial and the imagetic, contemporary architecture incurred a double and abominable deviation: On the one hand (i.e., from the perspective of the historical development), it ignored some of modernism's main achievements, especially the emphasis on the tension (pivotal to the work of Le Corbusier) between the phenomenological experience of real space and the superficial,

---

optical effects of façade plans and elevations (in the words of Colin Rowe and Robert Slutzky,[7] the tension between literal and phenomenal transparency); on the other hand (that is, from the perspective of postmodernist art practices), contemporary architecture has turned its back to what, especially with minimalism, has become the central motivation of the neo-avant-garde – i.e. the "structuring of materials in order to motivate a body and to demarcate a place."[8]

Foster's predilection for minimalism (to the detriment of pop art and most of all conceptual art) is not fortuitous, therefore. For, as he believes, it is due to minimalism the feat of turning the ideal object (i.e., amenable to a contemplative, sublime aesthetical experience) into a phenomenological object, that is one that can only be seized in the contingency of the lifeworld. In fact, Foster claims, if minimalism had performed a reduction to basic geometrical shapes, this was only "to prepare a sustained complexity, in which any ideality of form (which is thought to be instantaneous, even transcendental, in conception) is challenged by the contingency of perception (which occurs in particular bodies in specific spaces for various durations)".[9]

Thus, Foster's central thesis is that the art-architecture complex could be summarized today by a radical, and wholly regrettable, reversal of roles: Whereas, in Foster's words, "minimalists opened the art object to its architectural condition,"[10] contemporary architecture allowed buildings to be reduced to their superficial and imagistic condition – briefly, to mere appearance.

A good example of this type of reversal is the architecture of the duo Herzog & De Meuron. With a background of direct contact with neo-avant-garde practices, these architects occasionally gave in to the aesthetics of the superficial, the immaterial, and the atmospheric; in doing so, they relinquished their early commitment to matter, body, and place, producing instead an architecture in which matter turns to image, active perception turns to passive reception, and places turn to non-places. As becomes clear, the inordinate emphasis *The Art-Architecture Complex* imparts to the work of sculptor Richard Serra is not without justification:

AS FOSTER SEES IT, SERRA'S WORK EMBODIES WHAT IS MOST POWERFUL AND RESISTANT ABOUT BOTH CONTEMPORARY ART AND CONTEMPORARY ARCHITECTURE – NAMELY THE COMMITMENT TO THE MATTER-BODY-PLACE TRIAD.

In effect, Foster claims Serra's sculpture stand on three basic principles: a) the principle of material transparency (hence not only his choice of raw materials such as lead and steel, but also the precept that these should be tensed up through pertinent procedures); b) the phenomenological principle, i.e. the option for a sculpture that "exists in primary relation to the body, not as its representation but as its activation;" c) the situational principle, according to which "sculpture engages the particularity of place, not the abstraction of space."[11]

Were this text exclusively focused on the dilemmas and contradictions of contemporary art and art criticism, I would find myself obliged to extend upon the numerous flaws of Foster's reading – namely with regards to the definition of minimalism. Since this is not the case,[12] I will turn my attention now to the architectural shortcomings of Foster's approach. They are several and also very meaningful, the main one being the flagrant omissions of his book.

I am not referring to the fact that Foster operates with a restricted number of architectural practices; nor to the emphasis he gives to practices that best suit his line of thinking. No, first and foremost, I am thinking about the way Foster shunned the task of accounting for the practices and discourses which, as I see it, best represent the current state of the art-architecture complex – beginning with the works of Peter Eisenman and Rem Koolhaas.

This is not to say these architects are simply absent in *The Art-Architecture Complex*. They are not. However, their presence here takes on an alibi-like air – like a preventative defense against eventual accusations of neglect. Consider the case of Koolhaas. Although he is mentioned a dozen times throughout the book,

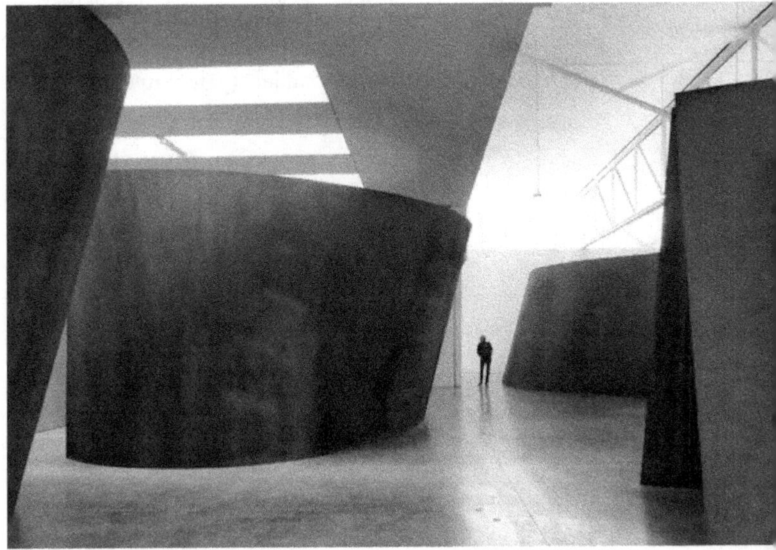

Richard Serra. Galeria Gagosian, Nova York NY , May 2010.

Photo Otavio Leonidio

Foster never addresses what is really crucial in his work – namely the way functionalism adresses the pair program-form. Instead, Foster's account is limited to short, anecdotal remarks – even to platitudes such as "the profile [of the Chinese Central Television siege] is motivated by the program, especially in the penultimate level that contains a great spiral of ramped bookshelves."[13]

Eisenman's case is even more problematic. For his presence here is not only precarious; it is contradictory. Indeed, although Foster admits that Eisenman carried out an unprecedented displacement of the subject (patent in the way the authorial subject is neutralized, particularly in his earlier projects), he never gives Eisenman's work the attention it deserves.[14]

For someone who claims, and solemnly so, that what is "at stake here are not mere preferences in design but important implications for subjectivity and society alike,"[15] this is a serious omission.

And that is not all, for Foster is obviously aware that since the mid-1960s (i.e., at the exact point when minimalism emerges), Eisenman has based his theoretical work on the dialogue with avant-garde art – particularly minimalism and conceptual art. Which means to say that – whether Foster likes it or not – the work of Eisenman incarnates the art-architecture complex to an extent that possibly trumps any other contemporary practice.

Eisenman's theoretical *oeuvre* confirms this. Consider, for instance, "Notes on Conceptual Architecture: Toward a Definition," an essay Eisenman published in 1971. As emphasized by the text's title, Eisenman main reference here is one of the most emblematic texts from 1960s aesthetical discourse: "Paragraphs on Conceptual Art," published by Sol LeWitt in 1967.[16] Moreover, as the reader soon realizes, Eisenman is particularly eager here to converse with other contemporary artists and theoreticians – namely, Donald Judd, Robert Morris, and Lucy Lippard. [17]

But "Notes on Conceptual Architecture" evidences much more than Eisenman's willingness to dialogue with 1960s avant-garde art; the text makes clear how original, and in a sense marginal, Eisenman's approach is. Two particular aspects are noteworthy in this respect. First, it springs to attention how young Eisenman resists accepting the (appealing and prevailing) conceptual/mental versus perceptual/phenomenological antinomy. Eloquently, Eisenman cautions that "[b]ecause the distinction between deep and surface, conceptual and perceptual, has not been clearly made, there remains a confusion between aesthetic and formal considerations." Thus, he concludes, "a problem remains as to what role these formal and essentially syntactic considerations must play if there is to be a conceptual aspect to architecture in built form."[18]

The second aspect (directly tied to the first) concerns Eisenman's reading of 1960s American art, especially minimalism. For Eisenman's conception of minimalism is radically different from Foster's; to his mind, minimalism operates a displacement from a 'primary experience which is visual and sensual' towards a "mental and intellectual and therefore presumed to be conceptual" experience, and not the other way around.[19] Which means to say that, just like Joseph Kosuth (and contrary to Foster),[20] Eisenman interprets minimalism from an anti-phenomenological perspective.[21]

Eisenman's special interest in the work of Sol LeWitt (to the detriment of Donald Judd and Robert Morris, arguably the primary ideologues of minimalism and post-minimalism, respectively) seems, in this sense, at once logical and strategical. Why? Because more than in any of his minimalist peers, in LeWitt's work antinomies such as conceptual versus perceptual and mental versus phenomenological are always called into question. In effect, in LeWitt's work these domains come together in a way that defies categorical polarizations. That Eisenman sees LeWitt's work this way becomes clear when he cautions:

Rosalind Krauss says that the LeWitt boxes and grids are not meant as physical things but as intellectual integers whose real existence is mental. She says that his implied argument that meanings are mental entities which somehow attach themselves to real objects is philosophically naïve. If the argument is phrased that meanings are *only* mental entities rather than *can be* mental entities, then she seems to have a valid position.[22]

The passage is rather telegraphical, but Eisenman's core argument is unequivocal: It concerns the constitution of meaning, more specifically the connection between a mental entity or event (i.e. an artist/architect's intention to produce something, in this case an art object or a building) and the meaning this thing eventually acquires for its viewers. Ultimately, therefore, what is at stake for Eisenman is the pertinence of artistic and architectural regimes of production eager to explore the connections between subjective intention, intellection processes, and phenomenological experience. Significantly, intentionality constitutes perhaps the primary theoretical problem of "Notes on Conceptual Architecture." The text's conclusion, in particular, makes this quite clear:

In summation, this paper has proposed a taxonomy that initially distinguishes between pragmatics, semantics, and syntactics.

Further, a distinction has been made between the perceptual
and conceptual aspects of each category. This distinction
was defined in each case by determining first the primacy of
intention, and second, the means used to articulate this intention.
In general, the conceptual aspect is defined by an intention
to shift the primary focus from the sensual aspects of objects
to the universal aspects of objects. This conceptual aspect to
be primary must be made intentional, that is, the result of an a
priori design intention, and further it must be accessible through
the physical fact— whether the primary intention is semantic
(concerned with meaning) or syntactic (concerned with formal
universals). And, finally, a further distinction was made in the
conceptual syntactic domain—between those aspects which
relied on formal universals to provide the conceptual aspect,
and those aspects which relied on a code or notational system.[23]

Now from the standpoint of the intention that underlies
the artistic/projective action, Eisenman's caveat to Krauss'
argumentation seems particularly relevant. For his interest
in the connections between an a priori design intention and
the intellection/experience of the physical fact underscores
a significant divergence *vis-à-vis* the foundations of one of
the most influential interpretations of contemporary art – an

interpretation whose foremost ideologue is Krauss, and one of the leading inheritors is Foster. What does this interpretations say? As per its most accomplished formulation (the essay "Sense and Sensibility. Reflection on Post '60s art," published by Krauss in 1973), basically this: 1) that all intention originates from a subjective and inscrutable mental space – in Krauss' words, "the artist inviolable self;" 2) that consequently, all art derived from the notion of intention will always be a) solipsistic and self-referential (in the sense that it will never retain any tangible and therefore verifiable connection with what supposedly originated it, and that its meaning will never transcend an act of imagination confined "to the mind of each isolated spectator"); b) prearranged (in the sense that it will always be the re-presentation of something formulated beforehand in the subject's conscience); c) conservative, in the sense that it will always reproduce a pre-defined and conventional formal/spatial model of some sort.[24]

Now, it was upon these presumption that Krauss would base her argument that American avant-garde art of the 1960s could be divided in two, and only two, opposing fronts – namely: a) the anti-intentional/progressive front constituted by both minimalism art and the non-conceptual section of post-minimalism; and b) the intentional/conservative front constituted by conceptual art (the art of Joseph Kosuth, On Kawara, and Douglas Huebler, among others).[25]

One understands why Krauss, like Foster, would pick Serra as one of the avatars of the non-conservative section of contemporary art: More than any one of his post-minimalist peers, Serra had always rejected any sort of a priori design intention and committed himself entirely to the body. Not any body, to be sure, but a body entirely aloof to all forms of subjective intention; a body which, in practice, does not avail itself to doing anything else except testing the properties of matter, investigating the possibilities of its own gestures in interacting with matter under the effect of gravity, seeking to define "the topology of the place, and the assessment of the characteristics of the place, through locomotion."[26] In praising Serra's phenomenological sculpture, Foster is merely echoing what Krauss had done 40 years before him.

But it can be misleading to emphasize the affinities between Foster's and Krauss' readings (in particular, the huge distrust both critics show for the conceptual/mental domain – a distrust always accompanied by a more or less unlimited faith in the virtues of the phenomenological experience). For there is something in *The Art-Architecture Complex* that sets it apart from the Krauss' highly ingenious reading of the art of the

1960s and afterward – namely an undisguisable unwillingness to develop, expose, and eventually test out the presumptions of his reading of the contemporary, especially the presumptions that underpin the imagistic/virtual versus real/phenomenological antinomy. In effect, notably when compared with Krauss' highly elaborate theoretical constructs, Foster's argumentation begins to resemble a short-circuit: instead of the complex articulation of conceptual-intencional-subjective-solipsistic-aprioristic-inscrutable-illusionistic-conventional-conservative, Foster bases his theses in the supposedly self-evident sequence: imagistic = virtual = illusory = acritical. It is a compromising shortcut; it suggests that, faced with the challenges and predicaments inherent in complex theoretical construction, Foster made a choice for moral judgment – or, worse still, moralist indictment. Personally, I believe this is precisely what Foster did when he implied that the path followed by Serra is evidently correct; that such a choice in fact constitutes an ineluctable antidote against all that is acritical/conservative in the contemporary world – especially that which he dubs (and quite infamously so) "the vicissitudes of the imaginary."[27] In doing so, Foster obliterates a significant number of questions – for instance, the problems and limitations that characterize the phenomenological model (which is actually presented here as problem-free). One of the risks involved is the incautious reader, and above all the neophyte, end up believing that, as Foster implies, Serra simply solved the problem of intentional/projective action (in his own words, "[h]ow might one proceed differently, sculpturally");[28] and that, as a consequence, his work constitutes an uncontroversial model to be followed by artists (but also by architects) intent on acting/designing in a non-conservative way.

That Foster has chosen not to pay Peter Eisenman's work the attention it deserves makes complete sense, on that account. After all from Eisenman's perspective (more specifically, as per his reading of 60s art), none of Foster's premises and contentions seem self-evident – quite the opposite. Which means to say that, if Foster deviated from Eisenman's work, he probably did so with the intent of obfuscating a work that challenges not only his outline of contemporary architecture, but first and foremost the foundations of his conception of the contemporary – namely: a) the idea that contemporary art and architecture can be characterized in terms of the opposition between, on the one hand, an imagistic/virtual domain (regarded as unrealistic and conservative) and, on the other hand, a phenomenological domain (seen as essentially real and progressive); b) that, therefore, the progressive choice among these two – and only two – alternatives can only be the option for the mundane/phenomenological, i.e. for the materic, the corporeal, the situational. To my mind, much of what Eisenman has been doing since the 1960s is aimed at challenging these precepts.

Obviously, by saying this I do not mean to imply that Eisenman simply solved the numerous problems his work raises – in particular the problem of the connections between subjective intention, intellection processes, and phenomenological experience. As a matter of fact, one of the distinctive features of his work is precisely a high degree of hesitance – particularly regarding the efficacy of his "architecture machine,"[29] both from the perspective of intentional action (i.e. regarding the attempted neutralization of a designer who acts driven by subjective/projective intentions) and from the perspective of intellection/experience (i.e. regarding the eventual overcoming of what he sharply denominates the "metaphysics of presence").[30] And the first one to admit this hesitance is Eisenman himself, who, after nearly half a century of work, continues to wonder: "How do you install the experience of the body and keep the mechanism operating?"[31]

But hesitance does not mean going backwards, let alone feeling nostalgic. Incidentally, Eisenman has always refused –

even at moments of great difficulty (for example when Derrida, rather surreptitiously, turned his back on him)[32] – accepting alternatives that suggested some sort of return to the pre-contemporary (which in his case means pre-deconstructivist) condition. Eisenman made this much clear when he stated, with an uncommon dose of sarcasm:

Our only source of value today is a memory of value, a nostalgia; we live in a relativistic world, yet desire absolute substance, something that is incontrovertibly real. Through its being, architecture has become, in the unconscious of society, the promise of this something real.[33]

It is unlikely that Eisenman had Foster in mind when he affirmed that; and yet it fits Foster like a glove. For as far as I see it, Foster is clearly after this unequivocal real. And just as this quest led him to Serra (the most mundane of all mundane artists), it also led him to architecture. Not just any architecture, but an architecture which, by definition, should be literal and never virtual; which is construction, rather than mere representation; which, in opposition to the work of the architects criticized in *The Art-Architecture Complex*, is made of literal transparencies, true phenomenological experiences, essential ties with specific places: In a word, an architecture that is always defined, and furthermore legitimized, by presence.

And this is the reason why, as I believe, Foster's account of contemporary architecture is less concerned with the art-architecture complex than it is with the challenges and dilemmas underlining a certain conception of contemporary art. What challenges are these? Above all, those associated with the problem of how one positions oneself in the face of what Hans U. Gumbrecht refers to as the unresolved crisis of metaphysics. In *The Return of the Real*, Foster seemed to wallow in an epistemological limbo of sorts: On the one hand, he disclosed an unrestrained desire for *the real*; on the other hand, he simply could not conceal his own ill-being in face of the very notion of reality – at least those notions of reality which, deliberately or not, might evoke a minimally stable form of referentiality (and ultimately, some sort of ontology). Hence, his caveat about the limits of his own intellectual endeavor, destined to reclaim not just any real, only a subjective reconstruction of it.[34] Eloquently, in the final chapter of *The Return of the Real*, Foster inquired about the deconstructions carried out by Foucault and Derrida:

Do these poststructuralisms elaborate the events of the postcolonial and the postmodern critically? Or do they serve as ruses whereby these events are sublimated, displaced, or otherwise effused? Or do they somehow do both?[35]

What was presented as doubt in *The Return of the Real* is taken for granted in *The Art-Architecture Complex*: The meaning of deconstruction becomes simply that of complicity, cynicism, the renouncing of critique. Likewise, the idea of a critical stance is now restricted to the option (presented as self-evident and self-justified) of returning to things themselves, to the presence of things themselves, to the grace that eventually arises in the presence of things themselves.

That Foster ends up attributing to the presence of some of Serra's works the quality of grace[36] (a word that has been banned from the avant-garde vocabulary since Michael Fried, in his infamous diatribe against minimal art, pronounced in 1967 the statement *presentness is grace*) seems highly symptomatic to me; it indicates the amount of conservativeness that underlies Foster's supposedly progressive critical praxis.

This conservativeness is not new. In fact, it is intrinsic to the notions of neo-avant-garde upon which Foster has built his alternative theory of the contemporary.[37] With this *The Art-Architecture Complex*, however, it took on clearer – and much more radical – contours.

**FOR WHAT THIS BOOK ULTIMATELY REVEALS
IS IN FACT THE HIGH DEGREE OF NOSTALGIA
THAT UNDERLIES FOSTER'S REASONING.**

Nostalgia of what? Now, nostalgia of the modern reality – i.e., of an aesthetical and existential condition which, as 1960s art makes clear (pace Foster), is not tenable anymore.

More specifically, Foster seems overrun with nostalgia of an age in which the avant-garde was driven by concrete causes (the quest for the lifeworld, the paving of the road to the future) which were acted out against concrete enemies (idealism, illusionism, pictorialism, etc.). In one word, what Foster misses is the same thing Fried could never find in minimal art – namely a "compelling conviction"[38] without which the modern spirit becomes homeless.

The end of this condition is experienced by Foster in eschatological terms – i.e., as the end of the world itself; like Fried and Krauss before him, Foster wound up incarnating what he quite accurately dubbed "the frightening of art and criticism" – i.e. the fear that the conditions on which for more than a century art and art criticism had been practiced and valued might come to an end.[39]

What does one do in the face of this terrifying scenario? One tries to demonstrate that, instead of the extinction of the modern condition, the contemporary world is actually a reconfiguration of it.

One evidence that this, in fact, is what drives Foster's critique is the emphasis *The Art-Architecture Complex* places upon the notion of virtual. As aforementioned, this term is employed here as the opposite of the articulated notions of concrete, real, mundane, tectonic, materic, etc. This antinomy is certainly not absurd; yet the way it is employed by Foster is somewhat shrewd. For as per Foster's critique, the notion becomes a contemporary, obvious equivalent to pre-modern notions such as ideal and illusionistic. The shrewdness lies in making believe that while the terms of the old antinomy ideal/classical versus mundane/modern may change, the antinomy itself remains ever current. Significantly, Foster recurrently describes the contemporary condition in terms of the old (i.e. modern) opposition between the real world versus the idealist world – as if implying that, like in the good old days of the avant-garde, our current predicament is still to confront "old idealist models."[40] In doing so, Foster not only suggests the persistence of the modern condition (now reconfigured); he insinuates that today, like yesterday, the task of the *neo-neo-avant-garde* is to fight "these persistent idealisms,"[41] now incarnated into an endless array of virtualities.

The shortcomings of this updating of the modern condition into the space of the contemporary are many. Let me highlight just one of them: How is one to account for practices that fit neither the original model (i.e., the modernist narratives), nor the reconfigured model (the neo-modernist ones) – as in the case, for example, of Robert Smithson?

Once again, Foster's solution brings Krauss to mind. For just like Krauss did repeatedly, Foster addresses the work of Smithson in eminently phenomenological terms – more specifically as per the purported emphasis his work gives to the notion of place.

To observers minimally familiar with the work of Smithson, the rationale sounds clumsy, for it conspicuously disregards the evidence that even when they take on a site-specific aspect, Smithson's works never cease to be the opposite of that, i.e. exemplars of an art that is anti-specific, anti-situational and anti-phenomenological.

Since Foster, like Krauss, simply cannot afford to leave Smithson outside the boundaries of the contemporary, all that is left for him is to try to replicate what Krauss had already done, and reasonably successfully so – namely approaching Smithson's work in essentially phenomenological terms, thus associating his earthworks with the situational operations of Andre, Serra, and Heizer.[42]

The gesture is unconvincing, but it serves as a lesson. For if it is still the time to look into the art of the 1960s, it is equally the time to question post-minimalist readings of this art – readings which, as Joseph Kosuth claimed were often moved by obscure agendas; readings which, as Foster's critique make explicit, have a huge impact in the way we deal with contemporary architecture.

Here again, Eisenman's legacy proves to be timely and strategic. For the fact that he is an utterly first-hand observer (and furthermore an original and independent observer) allowed him to impart a very special approach to 1960s art, notably regarding the – extremely sensitive – theme of intentionality. Significantly, instead of turning his back on the notion of intention (as Krauss[43] vehemently advised in the early 1970s), Eisenman persisted in his quest for what he inspiringly called "meta-intentionality."[44]

A circumstantiated analysis of this notion would require another paper. For the time being I will simply point out that, as Eisenman stated, such a notion puts the author in the precarious space which lies suspended in between the human and the inhuman – a space where modern subjectivity in general and critical judgment in particular become (in a best-case scenario) dysfunctional. Once again, it is worthwhile to resort to the words of Eisenman:

my work is ultimately about conceptualizing other methods. That is why I started working with other methods because all we can do as humans is to draw axes and places. The computer conceptualizes and draws differently... I attempt to remain suspended between the mechanism and my own subjective responses so that I am not able to define critically what its mistakes are in terms of the total trajectory of the work.[45]

To what extent does Eisenman's meta-intentionality intersect with minimalism's account of intention? This is the sort of question that remains unanswered – and which *The Art-Architecture Complex* has refrained from tackling. In any case, it is clear that while it is true that from Foster's neo-modernist standpoint "there are no alternatives without 'critique,'" it is also true that from an anti-modernist standpoint, critique may not be the best of alternatives – perhaps just the opposite.

Much has been said over the past few decades about the emergence (since around the mid-1960s) of a new agenda for architecture.[46] For the time being, this seems as encompassing as it is diffuse; it spans from semiotics to historicism, from environmentalism to feminism, from critical regionalism to deconstruction. Naturally, it also comprises the nexus art and architecture. Not by chance, alongside more or less commonplace topics such as "local tradition" and "sustainability," the métier of architecture has come to deal more recently with notions such as "field condition"[47] and "expanded field."[48] What is specific and interesting about the use of these notions is this: As their own champions recognize, they emulate the critical vocabulary of contemporary visual arts.

Obviously, there is nothing reproachable about architects employing notions and concepts imported from the discourse of the visual arts. My personal impression, however, is that as a rule, whenever architects utters an expression like "architecture's expanded field," they overlook the fact (rather obvious, by the way) that this and other notions were originally coined in specific contexts, that is to say as a reply to specific (aesthetical, but also political) questions and dilemmas.

In embracing these notions at face value, these architects do more than simply showing a greater or lesser degree of epistemological naiveté – or worse still, a greater or lesser degree of intellectual servility (which would imply that the current state of the art-architecture complex includes perhaps an inferiority complex on the part of architecture); they also disregard the fact that the decontextualized import of these notions can prove not only awkward, but unproductive as well. That is, in this case a minimum amount of deconstruction is not only recommended, it is actually a precondition for a freer and more productive exchange between art and architecture.

The elucidation of the current art-architecture complex must begin with this realization.

NOTES

AN. Many thanks to Francisco Lucena and Maria Palmeiro for their comments on this essay.

EN. Article previously published at: Otavio Leonidio, "O complexo Foster-Eisenman," *V!RUS* 12, 2016, www.nomads.usp.br/virus/virus12/?-sec=4&item=2&lang=pt.

1. Hal Foster, *The Art-Architecture Complex* (London/New York: Verso, 2011), XIII.

2. Hal Foster, *The Return of the Real* (Cambridge: The MIT Press, 1996).

3. Foster, *The Art-Architecture*, 83.

4. Ibid., 95.

5. Ibid., 96. In Foster's words, "In phenomenology the world is bracketed in such a way that what is primary in our experience comes to the fore". Ibid., 209.

6. In contrast with a "phenomenology [which] is shot through with pictures". Ibid., 124.

---

7. Colin Rowe and Robert Slutzky, "Transparency: Literal and Phenomenal," *Perspecta* 8, 1963, 45-54.

8. Foster, *The Art-Architecture*, 140-141.

9. Ibid., 107.

10. Ibid., VIII.

11. Ibid., 140.

12. I did this in: Otavio Leonidio, "O real e a história," *Novos Estudos Cebrap* 101, January/March, 2015, 178-182.

13. Foster, *The Art-Architecture*, 12.

14. Ibid., 84-85.

15. Ibid., 128.

16. Sol Lewitt, "Paragraphs on Conceptual Art," *Artforum* special issue, Summer 1967.

17. Peter Eisenman, "Notes on Conceptual Architecture: Toward a Definition," in Peter Eisenman, *Eisenman Inside Out: Selected Writings, 1963-1988* (New Haven/London: Yale University Press, 2004), 10-27.

18. Ibid., 27.

19. Ibid., 13.

20. See Joseph Kosuth, "History for," in Joseph Kosuth, *Art after philosophy and after: Collected Writing 1966-1990* (Cambridge: The MIT Press, 1991), 240.

21. Eloquently, Eisenman asserts that "It would seem that the idea of conceptual art would be to reveal something new in the mind, through

THE FOSTER-EISENMAN COMPLEX ___________________________

the physical form, rather than to explicitly reveal the concept, not through the form, but as the form. This idea would represent a problem for the work of Judd and Morris which again does not try to distinguish between a surface and a deep structure within the object." Eisenman, "Notes on Conceptual Architecture," 26

22. Ibid., 25.

23. Ibid., 23.

24. Rosalind Krauss, "Sense and Sensibility: Reflection on Post '60s Sculpture," *Artforum*, v. 12, n. 3, November 1973, 43-53.

25. In fact, according with Krauss (1973), the meaning of minimalist art is not essentially different from the meaning of post-minimalist art, since both abdicated of all kind of intentionality.

26. Richard Serra, *Writings/Interviews* (Chicago: The University of Chicago Press, 1994), 15.

27. Foster, *The Art-Architecture*, 127.

28. Ibid., 136.

29. Peter Eisenman, "A Conversation with Peter Eisenman," *El Croquis* 83, 1997, 19.

30. Peter Eisenman, "Presentness and the Being-Only-Once of Architecture," in Peter Eisenman, *Written into the Void: Selected Writings. 1990-2004* (New Haven/London: Yale University Press, 2007), 42-49.

31. Eisenman, "A Conversation," 14.

32. Peter Eisenman, "Post/El Cards. A Reply to Jacques Derrida," in Eisenman, *Written into the Void*, 1-5.

33. Peter Eisenman, "Architecture and the Problem of the Rhetorical Figure," in Eisenman, *Eisenman Inside Out*, 203.

34. Foster, *The Return*, 239. In its original formulations, the restriction was even more rigorous: "Repressed by various poststructuralisms, the real has returned - but not just any real, onlye the traumatic real. Hal Foster, "What's Neo about the Neo-Avant-Garde?," *October* 70, Fall 1994, 29.

35. Foster, *The Return*, 217.

36. Foster, *The Art-Architecture*, 157.

37. Leonidio, "O real e a história."

38. Michael Fried, "Art and Objecthood," *Artforum*, Summer 1967, 12-23.

39. Hal Foster, "Art critics in extremis," in Hal Foster, *Design and Crime (and Other Diatribes)* (London/New York: Verso, 2003), 117.

40. Foster, *The Art-Architecture*, 145.

41. Ibid., 146.

42. Ibid., 138. See Craig Owens, "Earthwords," *October* 10, Fall 1979, 121-130.

43. Krauss, "Sense and Sensibility."

44. Eisenman, "A Conversation," 17.

45. Ibid., 13.

46. *Theorizing a New Agenda for Architecture: An Anthology of Archi-*

THE FOSTER-EISENMAN COMPLEX

tectural Theory, 1965-1995, ed. Kate Nesbitt (New York: Princeton Architectural Press, 1996).

47. Stan Allen, "Junkspace," in *Constructing a New Agenda: Architectural Theory 1993-2009*, ed. A. Krista Sykes (New York: Princeton Architectural Press, 2010).

48. Anthony Vidler, "Architecture by Numbers", in *Constructing a New Agenda*.

GUY DEBORD AND ROBERT SMITHSON

SPACE, TIME, AND HISTORY

TRANSLATED BY GIOVANA SANCHEZ

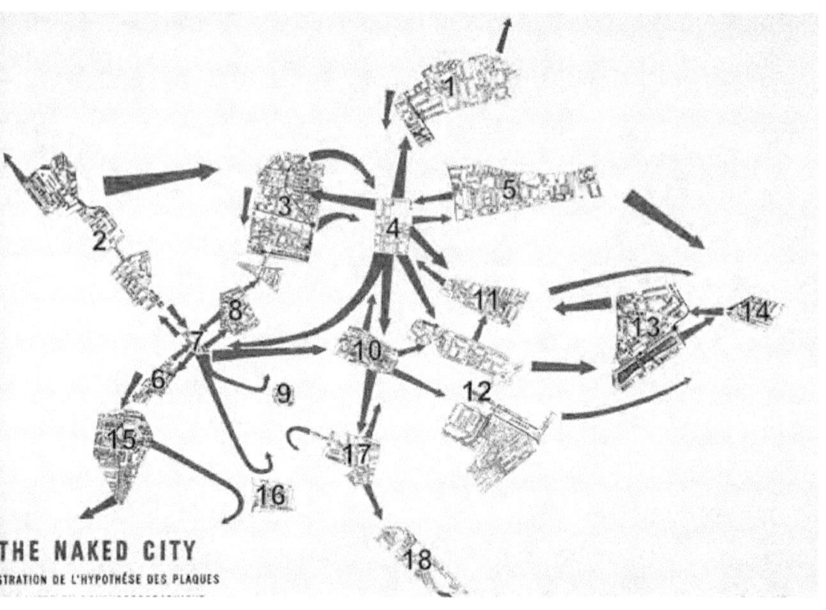

The Naked City. Guy Debord, 1957

But who will come and from where?

Federico Garcia Lorca, *Somnambule Ballad.*

The Naked City is perhaps the most famous exemplar of a situationist psychogeographical map.[1] The map is a collage of 18 cutouts, drawn from a conventional map of the city of Paris and freely rearranged throughout the new chart. It also comprises 46 arrows of different sizes and shapes. According to its author, the French activist Guy Debord (Paris, 1931 – Bellevue-la-Montagne, 1994) the cutouts represent "unities of ambiance" or "of atmosphere," defined not by administrative boundaries but by the affection, passion and intuition of Paris residents. The arrows in turn represent "principal axes of passage" and "directions of penetration" which, in psychogeographical terms, supposedly interconnect these different unities of ambience.[2]

Clearly, the purpose of the map is to illustrate two distinct yet interrelated phenomena: a) the set of urban units purportedly endowed with a more or less homogeneous character; and b) the unusual interconnections defined by an alternative experience of public space – more precisely, the experience provided to "one or more persons [who] during a certain period drop their relations, their work and leisure activities, and all their other usual motives for movement and action, and let themselves be

---

drawn by the attractions of the terrain and the encounters they find there."[3] In short, the map is the expression of an alternative Paris, one that is mentally constructed by an array of *dérives* (drifts) – according to the situationist definition, "a technique of rapid passage through varied ambiances."[4]

Regardless of its unusual aspect, *The Naked City* does not infringe the principles of conventional cartography: As with traditional maps, it intends to be an accurate representation of a specific topography. Only, instead of the *real* urban morphology it seeks to represent the topography of the Paris that exist inside the mental space of its residents. The outcome might seem unconventional but it is not properly arbitrary or altogether subjective. As a metter of fact, it aims to be an objective representation of a subjective reality. To a large extent, thus, *The Naked City* is the product of the same scientific motivation inherent in the production of traditional maps. And the first to acknowledge that is Debord himself. In his words, the *dérives* and their cartographic representation integrate "the study of the exact laws and specific effects of geographical environments, whether consciously organized or not, on the emotions and behavior of individuals."[5]

The apparent disorder of *The Naked City* is also deceptive. The map is the illustration of a fairly schematic idea – one that is based on the categorical opposition between, on the one hand, notions

GUY DEBORD

AND ROBERT SMITHSON

such as identity and autonomy, and on the other hand, integration and connectivity. *The Naked City* is not just a conventional illustration; it is the conventional illustration of a conventional idea.

Something similar can be said of the formal aspect of the map; for it also follows a ratter rigorous and canonical ordering. Namely, the two set of graphic elements employed by Debord here (cutouts and arrows) had been conventionally laid out over the graphic space of the map – an arrangement that complies with precepts such as balance and hierarchical distribution of parts. Formally, *The Naked City* is a conventional, protocol device – one that abides by the precepts of classical composition.

But above all, *The Naked* reflects a glaring contradiction, namely between the unconventional attitude of the *real* urban space, and the conventional occupation of the map's graphic space. Put differently, if there is something that Debord never considered while drawing his map was to left himself adrift, to put himself in a estate of *dérive*. That is, and to quote Debord himself, he never confronted his own "motives for movement and action." On the contrary, the movements and actions in the origin of the map were seemingly guided by a rigorous, conventional form of spatial behavior – as highlighted above, inherited from classical tradition.

The need to confront one's "motives for movement and action" was a pressing question for an influential group of

---

contemporary artists. Artists such as Frank Stella and Donald Judd, among others, believed in fact that the setting of alternative justifications for their artistic actions were perhaps even more important than the products of these actions. What was at stake for these artists was the setting of non-compositional procedures – that is to say, apt to break free from the tenets of classical morphology (in particular, and to quote Stella, the precept according to which "you do something in one corner [of the canvas] and balance it with something in the other corner").[6]

In Stella's case, the answer to the question of how to act was required following the movements suggested, as it were, by the shape of the canvas itself. His famous black striped paintings of the late 1950s epitomize this anti-compositional behavior. A case in point is *Die Fahne Hoch!*, from 1959. As noted by Rosalind Krauss, the making of this painting (and of many others produced by Stella in the early 1960s) does not conform to traditional modes of composition; instead, they follow a deductive procedure – in the sense that "all internal differentiations of its surfaces derive from the literal aspects of the canvas edge."[7] In the specific case of *Die Fahne Hoch!*, once the midpoints of the four sides of the rectangle were established, Stella's actions were limited to forcing the stripes into a "repetitive, unbroken declaration of the expanse of the painting's four quadrants in a double set of mirror reversals."[8]

The same kind of self-restraint marks Judd's actions. In this case, however, the strategy was based on the repetition of a particular plastic element – a procedure synthetized by the famous motto, "one thing after another."[9] Eloquently, when he published his most famous and influential essay (*Specific Objects*, 1965), Judd quoted John Locke on the motives of human action: "The motive to change is always some uneasiness: nothing setting us upon the change of state, or upon any new action, but some uneasiness."[10]

PERSONALLY, I THINK THAT THE MOST INSPIRING SHARE OF NORTH AMERICAN (AND EVEN NON-NORTH AMERICAN) ART PRODUCED SINCE THE MID-1960S RESPONDS IN ONE WAY OR ANOTHER TO THIS ESSENTIAL QUESTION: HOW TO ACT?

Significantly, the motto was not restricted to painting or sculpture; it includes one of the most exciting forms of contemporary art: Performance. It is noteworthy, by the way – and this is especially interesting for us here – that some of the most emblematic performances of the 1960s and 70s were not enacted inside studios, galleries and museums, but in the public urban space. As such, they constitute exercises in urban spatial imagination.

A prominent example of one such action is *Following Piece*, performed in the streets of New York by Vito Acconci throughout an entire month, in October, 1969. At first glance, *Following Piece* resembles a situationist *dérive*. Acconci has described his performance as follows:

Each day I pick out, at random, a person walking in the street. I follow a different person everyday; I keep following until that person enters a private place (home, office, etc.) where I can't get in.[11]

Following Piece does not comprise the production of a map – and not without good reasons. After all, this performance does not seek to add any form of knowledge to the issues it addresses, namely to ways of occupying the urban public space. Instead, Acconci produced a "Diary of a body," in which he described – in the crudest possible way – what actually took place in each day of his performance. On October 3, the first day of the performance, the diary records:

9:12 AM, in front of door, 102 Christopher St, my home. Man in gray suit – he walks W on Christopher, S side of street./ 9:17AM: he gets into car parked outside post office, Christopher & Greenwich, and drives away.[12]

Later, on October 12, Acconci notes only: "I didn't follow anyone."[13]

But for at least one artist formed in the minimalist environment, the production of maps seemed mandatory: Robert Smithson.

As with the Situationist maps, Smithson's maps are related to the mental experiences of physical space. The similarities end here. For in contrast with a map like *The Naked City*, Smithson's maps were not meant to be realistic representations of the physical space. On the contrary, his maps are assumedly fictional, and are as disruptive as his famous site/non-site operations.

Indeed, Smithson's site/non-sites kept no realistic connections with the places they represented. Rather, they aimed to deconstruct the very notion of place. In an interview from the 1970s Smithson emphasized the corrosive aspect of his representation/intervation. "Although the nonsite designates the site," he stated, "the site itself is open and really unconfined and constantly being changed... the thing was to bring these two things together."[14]

In "A Provisional Theory of Non-Sites," Smithson clarified the differences between his maps[15] and conventional maps and other forms of planimetric representations:

By drawing a diagram, a ground plan of a house, a street plan to
the location of a site, or a topographic map, one draws a *logical
two dimensional picture*. A *logical picture* differs from a natural or
realistic picture in that it rarely looks like the thing it stands for.
It is a two dimensional analogy or metaphor – A is Z... A logical
intuition can develop in an entirely *new sense of metaphor* free
of natural of realistic expressive content. Between the actual
site in the Pine Barrens and *The Non-Site* itself exists a space of
metaphoric significance. It could be that *travel* in this space is a
vast metaphor. Everything between the two sites could become
physical metaphorical material devoid of natural meanings and
realistic assumptions. Let us say that one goes on a fictitious trip
if one decides to go to the site of the Non-Site.[16]

What should be emphasized here is not simply the abstract character of Smithson's maps, but rather the radical objection to the notion of real space. For Smithson, in fact, maps and
other representations of the physical space were no more fictional than the physical space itself. Thus, Smithson's maps do not
simply counter the principle of formal homology that governs
the preparation of conventional maps; they aim to displace its
users, enable them to get astray inside the voids they open in
between a site and a non-site.

That Smithson was apt to experience the world as if it were a giant map (a map in a 1:1 scale) is suggested by his description of his tour through the "Monuments of Passaic." In his words, this "fictional trip" had immersed him in an absurd spatiality, an "anti-romantic mise-en-scène" made of "dislocated directions" and "ruins in reverse" – a mirror structure that "kept changing places with the reflection."[17] As a matter of fact, Smithson claimed, he had not toured on the real Passaic," but "on a planet that had a map of Passaic drawn over it": "At any moment my feet were apt to fall through the cardboard ground."[18]

Smithson's account gives a good measure of how the artist moved and acted in the space of the world. And perhaps because he did in fact lived imersed in a giant fictional map, Smithson never called into question his own motives for movement and action. Smithson biggest contribution to the minimalist thinking is perhaps this: He removed the emphasis minimalist artists gave to justifications and placed it on the (as a rule naturalized) notions of event and action. Significantly, Smithson always mistrusted the notion of action – in particular, the engaged action.

A discussion between Smithson and Allan Kaprow (Atlantic City, 1927–Encinitas, 2006), published in 1967, heralds this essential aspect of his reasoning. Confronted by Kaprow's claim that "the concept of the museum is completely irrelevant" (in contrast to the socio-cultural environment that surround them) Smithson replied that "the nullity implied in the museum is actually one of its major assets, and... this should be realized and accentuated." Incidentally, he claimed, one of the greatest virtues of museums was the fact that they were "nullifying in regard to action."[19]

Smithson's irrepressible contempt for the notion of action can be idiosyncratic; it reflects at any rate the way artists formed in the minimalist tradition could deal with this critical issue. In this regard, what separates the Situationist action – in particular the dérive – from various forms of minimalist and post-minimalist actions is not, I think, merely the fact that "situationist drift did not intend to be seen as a proper artistic activity."[20] Rather, it is the constructive pathos that characterize Situationist actions, the fact that Situationist actions had always been conceived and performed (in contrast with minimalist actions) as means for future social transformation – in a word, as utopia.

Beyond different conceptions of art, this divergence points to a more essential contradiction – one that opposes the conflicting temporalities underlying the situationist and the minimalist worldviews.

AS THE PRODUCT OF THE MARXIST IDEOLOGY, DEBORD'S CONCEPT OF ACTION IS GUIDED BY A TYPICALLY HISTORICIST CONCEPT OF TEMPORAL TRANSITION.

Accordingly, human action is – and should always be – engaged in the development of what Reinhart Koselleck dubbed the collective singular "History," i.e. a general or global process that engulfs and interconnects what until the end of 18th century was perceived as a multitude of individual and self-sufficient histories. As per this new conception of history, the importance and the value of each and every action becomes literally relative and precarious, in the sense that it is understood and appraised in terms of the place these acts occupy in, and the role they play for, the development of "History."[21]

Debord's notion of innovative art is the product of this specific concept of history; it pretends that all forms of non-conservative action must be consciously engaged in the historical development. In effect, it presupposes something even more ambitious: the engagement in the revolutionary/utopian transformation of reality. As Debord wrote in one of his most emblematic essays,

---

the world must be changed. We want the most liberating
change of the society and life in which we find ourselves
confined. We know that such a change is possible through
appropriate actions.[22]

The notion of "appropriate action" is essential to Debord. He conceives it as an action that results from a rational and judicious evaluation of the current historical situation. Debord's critique of surrealism reflects this concept of appropriate action. To his mind, the great mistake of surrealism was to have bet on the "infinite richness of the unconscious." And according to Debord, "We need to make the world more rational — the necessary first step in making it more exciting, fascinating and fulfilling."[23] Therein, precisely, resided the strength and intelligence of the "collective vanguard" represented by situationism:

The very notion of a collective avant-garde, with the militant
aspect it implies, is a recent product of the historical conditions
that are simultaneously giving rise to the necessity for a
coherent revolutionary program in culture and to the necessity
to struggle against the forces that impede the development
of such a program. Such groups are led to transpose into their
sphere of activity certain organizational methods originally

created by revolutionary politics, and their action is henceforth

inconceivable without some connection with a political critique.

In this regard there is a notable progression from Futurism

through Dadaism and Surrealism to the movements formed

after 1945. At each of these stages, however, one discovers the

same desire for total change; and the same rapid disintegration

when the inability to change the real world profoundly enough

leads to a defensive withdrawal to the very doctrinal positions

whose inadequacy had just been revealed.[24]

> In this sense, too, *The Naked City* is a paradigmatic document.
> Because, as emphasized by Debord, this map is not an accom-
> plished representation of the situationist city (the city deconstruc-
> ted and reconstructed by multiple drifts) but solely a provisional
> version of it. Debord's justification for such precariousness was
> based on the evidence that, *so far*, all that could be done with the
> knowledge driven from multiple derives was the production of

lacking maps of influences, maps whose inevitable imprecision

at this early stage is no worse than that of the first navigational

charts. The only difference is that it is no longer a matter

of precisely delineating stable continents, but of changing

architecture and urbanism.[25]

Again, the comparison with Smithson is instructive. For if there is something that this artist viscerally abhorred was the idea of utopia. Such contempt was not unjustified. For

AS SMITHSON REALIZED, THE CONCEPT OF UTOPIA HAD ALWAYS BEEN LINKED[26] TO TEMPORAL CONSCIOUSNESS UNDERLYING THE HISTORICIST IDEOLOGY – MORE PRECISELY, HISTORICISM'S CONCEPTION OF AN OPEN AND INEXHAUSTIBLE FUTURE.[27]

In this sense, the difference between a map like *The Naked City* and Smithson's maps is not just the abstract spatiality that characterizes the later, but rather its absurd, shamelessly fictional and essentially anti-historicism temporality. Significantly, instead of unexpected connections between urban units of ambience,[28] Smithson's maps allude to absurd and paradoxical spatial – but also temporal – coexistences, to fictional worlds consisting of infinite multiplications and double identities, replicas and reflections, time oscillations and infinite multiplications.[29]

Accordingly, instead of a balanced composition of autonomous graphic elements, Smithson's maps are made of juxtapositions and overlaps, folds and cancellations, stacks and reflections. To say that these maps do not fit in the cartographical tradition is insufficient. As in the famous short story by Borges,[30] they conjure a temporality that does not fit in History.

NOTES

EN. Article previously published at: Otavio Leonidio, "Guy Debord e Robert Smithson. Espaço, tempo e história," *Arquitextos* 176.00, Vitruvius, January 2015, www.vitruvius.com.br/revistas/read/arquitextos/15.176/5458.

1. Paola Berenstein Jacques, "Breve histórico da Internacional Situacionista – IS," *Arquitextos* 035.05, Vitruvius, April 2003, www.vitruvius.com.br/revistas/read/arquitextos/03.035/696.

2. Guy Debord, "Teoria da deriva," trans. Carlos Roberto Monteiro de Andrade, *Óculum* 4, 1993, 26-29.

3. Ibid., 27.

4. Guy Debord, "Report on the Construction of Situations and on the International Situationist Tendency's Conditions of Organization and Action," *Situationist International Online*, June 1957, www.cddc.vt.edu/sionline/si/report.html.

5. Ibid.

6. Frank Stella, "Questions to Stella and Judd," in *Minimal Art: A Critical Anthology*, ed. Gregory Battcock (Nova York: E. P. Dutton, 1968).

Originally published at *Art News*, September 1966.

7. Rosalind Krauss, "Sense and Sensibility: Reflection on Post '60s Sculpture," *Artforum*, November 1973, 43-53.

8. Ibid.

9. Donald Judd, "Specific Objects," *Arts Yearbook* 8, 1965.

10. John Locke, *An essay concerning human understanding*, quoted in Judd, "Specific Objects."

11. Vito Acconci, *Diary of a body (1969-1973)* (Milão: Charta, 2006), 76.

12. Ibid., 78.

13. Ibid.

14. Robert Smithson, "Interview with Robert Smithson for the Archives of American Art/Smithsonian Institution," in *Robert Smithson. The Collected Writings*, ed. Jack Flam (Berkeley: University of California Press, 1996), 295.

15. "The nonsite exists as a kind of deep three dimensional abstract map that points to a specific site on the surface of the earth. And that's designated by a kind of mapping procedure... these places are not destinations; they kind of [are] backwaters or fringe areas". Ibid.

16. Robert Smithson, "A Provisional Theory of Non-Sites," in *Robert Smithson*, 364. Smithson's highlights.

17. Robert Smithson, "The Monuments of Passaic," *Artforum*, December 1967, 51.

18. Ibid., 50-51.

19. "What is a Museum," *Arts Yearbook* 9, 1967, 95.

20. Jacques, "Breve histórico."

21. See Reinhart Koselleck, "'Space of Experience' and 'Horizon of Expectation': two historical categories," in Reinhart Koselleck, *Futures Past: On the Semantics of Hstorical Times* (Nova York: Columbia University Press, 2004).

22. Debord, "Report on the Construction."

23. Ibid.

24. Ibid.

25. Debord, "Teoria da deriva," 28.

26. Miguel Abensour has been working with the concept of "persistent utopia", at the same time sympathetic and critic with the tradition of utopic thinking. I appreciate for Henrique Estrada calling my attention to Abensour's thinking.

27. Robert Smithson, "Ultramodern," *Arts Magazine* 42, September/October 1967, 31.

28. Debord, "Report on the Construction."

29. Smithson, "Ultramodern," 33.

30. Jorge Luis Borges, "O jardim dos caminhos que se bifurcam," in Jorge Luis Borges, *Ficções* (São Paulo: Globo, 1969).

HAL FOSTER
HISTORY AND THE REAL

TRANSLATED BY GABRIEL POMERANCBLUM

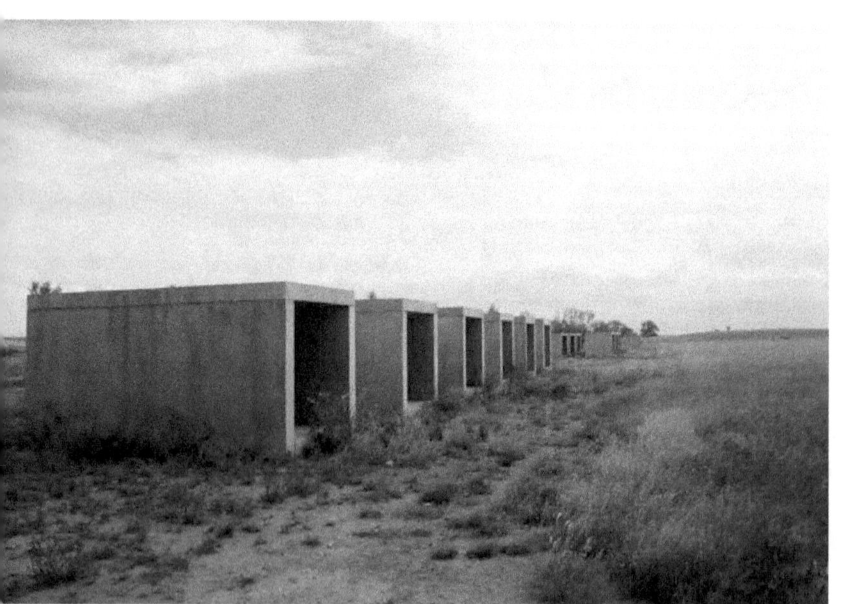

Donald Judd, Marfa TX, 2012. Photo Otavio Leonidio

The problems around which *The Return of the Real* is constituted are immense. They have nourished the thought and practice of critics and artists alike since the mid-1960s – that is, for half a century now; in one way or another, and particularly regarding the meaning of so-called contemporary art, they reflect a crucial question – namely, the crisis of the conception of history upon which art had been produced (and still is, at least partly) since romanticism. More pointedly, the core issue of *The Return of the Real* is the overcoming of a "persistent historicism that condemns contemporary art as belated, redundant, repetitious."[1] In large measure, therefore, Hal Foster is facing the same challenges and dilemmas as a generation of artists and critics who realized, as Robert Smithson had claimed, that "a transhistorical consciousness has emerged in the 1960s."[2]

Foster's agenda does not coincide, however, with that of 1960s artists. What is at stake for him is also, and perhaps above all else, the subsistence of a practice (art criticism) which, since romanticism, has placed the meaning of works of art in the juncture between the notion of aesthetical quality (tied to the transcendental notion of aesthetic experience) and the one of historical pertinence (tied in turn to the position these works occupy in, and the role they played for, the development of the history of art). In other words, what is at stake for Foster are the conditions of possibility of a critical discourse whose foundations to a large extent coincide with the advent (towards the end of 18th century) of historicism – precisely the foundations 1960s art had put in check. Which means to say that, in contrast with much of 1960s and 70s art, Foster is committed to safeguarding an important dimension of the modernist establishment. How so? By means of a "posthistorical account of the neo-avant-garde, as well as an eclectic notion of the postmodern."[3]

Foster's solution draws on the notion of neo-avant-garde, and even more so of deferred action. Borrowed from psychoanalytical theory, this last one pretends that "one event is only registered through another that recodes it; we come to be who we are only in deferred action (*Nachträglichkeit*)." The book's entire argumentation hinges in fact on the idea that "historical and neo-avant-gardes are constituted in a similar way, as a continual process of protension and retention, a complex relay of anticipated futures and reconstructed pasts."[4] The framework is strategic; it works as an antidote against the contention (put forth by Peter Bürger in *Theory of the Avant-Garde*, against which *The Return of the Real* was clearly written)[5] that 1960s art was nothing more than a farcical, acritical repetition of the actions undertaken by historical avant-gardes. For Foster, on the contrary, 1960s neo-avant-gardes amount to the full accomplishment of what had only incompletely been carried out in the early 20th century by movements such as Russian constructivism, De Stijl, dadaism and surrealism.

Of course, one can dispute the effectiveness of the psychoanalytical model adopted by Foster, that is to say argue whether or not it constitutes a de facto gain in the current understanding of 1960s art. Significantly so, the question is raised by Foster himself, who concedes that "even as I complicate development with deferred action, my extension of the (re)construction of the individual subject to the (re)construction of an historical subject is problematic." Hence the question: "Can I address the logic of the subject historically if my model of history presupposes this logic? Is this a productive double bind or a paralytic one?"[6]

The fact that Foster stuck to his psychoanalytic model (without which this book would not exist) doesn't mean he had put an end to the problem. In fact, epistemologically speaking, the book only lays bare the dilemmas of a generation of progressive intellectuals who, having come of age in an overtly deconstructivist environment, found themselves in the 1980s (that is, in a context where both AIDS and Reaganomics ran rampant and were met with no institutional resistance) seeking a less unrealistic theoretical apparatus than deconstructivism. Foster's caveat about the limits of his own intellectual endeavor (designed, as he cautions, to retrieve not reality as such, but only a subjective reconstruction of it)[7] sounds doubly symptomatic in this respect: On the one hand, it evinces an unrestrained yearning for the real; on the other, it unveils a persistent malaise *vis-à-vis* the very notion of the real – at least those notions of the real that might evoke the idea of a stable, substantial referentiality. More than a quandary, Foster's position exposes the aporetic condition of the *post*-postmodernist project, of which he is an avatar. Tellingly, in the final chapter of *The Return of the Real*, Foster wonders about the consequences of the deconstructions performed by Foucault and Derrida: "Do these poststructuralisms elaborate the events of the post-colonial and the postmodern critically? Or do they serve as ruses whereby these events are sublimated, displaced, or otherwise defused?"[8] Trapped inside an epistemological limbo-of-sorts,

FOSTER SEEKS SHELTER IN A POST-TRANSCENDENTAL WORLD THAT IS PARTICULARLY HOSTILE TO WORLDVIEWS THAT ARE EVEN SLIGHTLY SUBSTANTIALIST.[9]

But Foster's solution is not unfounded; just like Bürger he believes that the chief motivation of 1960s art was the recovery (seen as acritical and anachronistic by Bürger, and deliberate and opportune by Foster) of actions already performed by the "historical avant-garde." Indeed, as Foster put it, "artists in the 1960s had to elaborate [avant-garde devices] critically; the pressure of historical awareness permitted anything less."[10] This is, in fact, the undiscussed assumption of *The Return of the Real*, which simply takes for granted that the main goal of 60s art was to "refashio[n] avant-garde devices... to contemporary ends".[11] As is clear, Foster's objection to Bürger is only partial, the difference between both standings residing merely in how each interpreter assesses one and the same phenomenon – Foster extoling it while Bürger decries it.

The shortcomings of *The Return of the Real* are the product of that assumption, starting with the book's inability in accounting for the style Foster seems most affined with – minimalism. For while minimalism (and a considerable share of the art made in its wake) puts in check the notion of avant-garde (due, precisely, to the ties it keeps with the historicist worldview), Foster proves unable to conceive of any version of ambitious or challenging art which is not also advanced or innovative (and, accordingly, do not comply with notions such as development, advancement and progress). Put differently, what Foster (like Bürger) doesn't seem ready to conceive of, let alone accept, is – to quote TJ Clark – an art with no future.[12] Hence the mismatch: While a significant portion of 1960s and 1970s art sought to conjure up a metahistorical temporal experience (in whose context the notion of avant-garde simply makes no sense), Foster strives at all costs to preserve the "historicity of all art, including the contemporary."[13] Of course, together with such essential historicity, Foster is committed to preserve art's critical condition – or more pointedly, art's *historical* critical condition. Once again, we are faced with an axiomatic stance. For in Foster's eyes there simply is no criticality in a context characterized by "a relative inattention to the historicity of art" and a "loss of historical purchase."[14]

The modernist assumptions underlying this strive to safeguard art's – mandatory – historicity (and along with it a criticism allegedly based on a renewed concept of "historical development") are evident: Willfully or not, the main function of the notion of neo-avant-garde is to preserve "the tradition of the new" – that is to say, an aesthetical regimen of production according to which "having a place in art history is the value."[15]

Of course, Foster would not concur; he is convinced that his alternative model of historical development indeed complexities fundamental historicist categories such as causality, temporality, and narrativity;[16] that in doing so he has actually left behind historicism's characteristic concept of historical development. As far as I see it, however, Foster did not overcome the historicist model, only an oversimplified version of it.

Not that Foster ignores the complexity of the theoretical problems he is dealing with; in particular, he is aware of the protagonism that the notion of event takes on here – the fact that, as Slavoj Zizek cautions, "the crucial point here is the changed status of an event."[17] But here again the dialogue with Bürger proves harmful. Why? Because the notion of event Foster pretends to complexify, which he borrowed from Bürger, doesn't span much further than the Marxian boutade according to

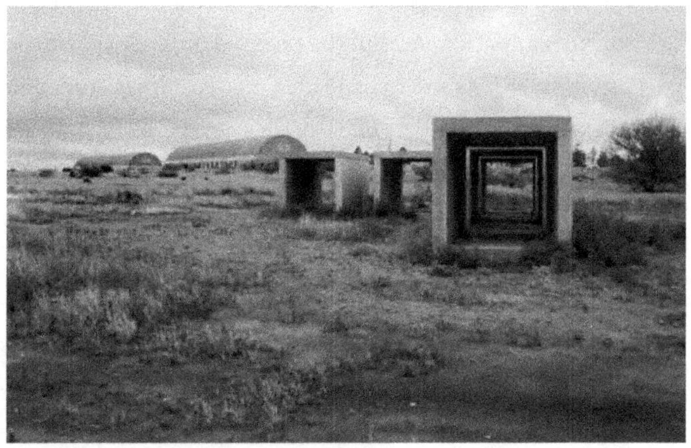

Donald Judd, Marfa TX, 2012. Photo Otavio Leonidio

which "all great events of world history occur twice, the first time as tragedy, the second time as farce." [18] Now by choosing as a reference such oversimplified notion of event, Foster disregards the evidence that the defining trait of the historicist notion of event is not singularity but rather instability, that is to say the fact that one such event is always prone to alter its identity, as a result of the changing status it acquires as history progresses.[19] The philosopher Hannah Arendt had also analyzed this peculiar aspect of the modern notion of event; and as she demonstrates, in an epistemological context dominated by the notion of process, "nothing is meaningful in and by itself, not even history or nature taken each as a whole, and certainly not particular occurrences in the physical order or specific historical events."[20] As is clear, the idea that Foster succeeded in complexifying the notions of event and development is misleading. What Foster complexified was a pair of stereotypes.

To have used as a reference such an oversimplified notion of event is not unjustified, though; for it perfectly suits an argumentation that no longer defines the neo-avant-garde as a farcical reenactment of their historical/authentic counterparts, but instead as their ultimate accomplishment. Once again, one sees how limited is Foster disagreement with Bürger. For his reading remains dependent upon the – typically modernist – notions, and even more so the correlate values, of authenticity and originality. After all, what is it that Foster intends to sustain through his alternative notions of event and historical development if not the thesis that the neo-avant-garde of the 1960s is *not* farcical and spurious? Foster's argumentation is indeed unambiguous: If the neo-avant-garde reenacts historical actions and events, it is due to the fact that (in line with the notion of "deferred action") their initial occurrences had been incipient, incomplete. That is, instead of a mere repetition, their second occurrence actually amounts to the release (and the full accomplishment) of something that had remained repressed for 30 or 40 years. What Foster propounds therefore is the thesis that, in conjunction with their historical counterpart, the belated actions of the neo-avant-garde amount to an event that is truly authentic and original. Now, shouldn't a truly non-historicistic stance, on the contrary, simply disregard the notions of authenticity and originality?

What Foster is unable to conceive of, on the other hand, is a concept of history that is not progressive and developmental, that is to say that does not progress toward historicism's notion of an open and inexhaustible future. As a typical historicist critic, he assumes that development is an insurmountable condition of temporal transition itself – and not a value entirely dependent on a specific and circumstantial concept of history.

That the defense of a renewed Marxism (in contrast to Bürger's ossified Marxism) is at the core of Foster's reflection is not fortuitous either: What is at stake for him is also the subsistence of a historically engaged art act – i.e. an act performed in the name of the historical development. For Foster, indeed, an ambitious art practice is, of necessity, tantamount to a historically-engaged practice. In other words, just as any other form of progressive action, the main purpose of the art act is help propelling the historical development. The assumption has a strong implication to criticism. After all, just as ambitious art has no place outside the historical development, the same holds true of ambitious criticism. This is in fact the primary function, and the main source of legitimacy, of avant-garde criticism, whose main function is the attribution of the historical situation of works of art, that is to say the place they occupy in the all-encompassing history of art. Foster doesn't recant the principle – on the contrary: In his words, as much as artistic praxis does, critical activity must follow the precept that "historical insight does not depend on contemporary advocacy, but an engagement in the present, whether artistic, theoretical, and/or political."[21]

But note that this principle suggests more than the need to engage in the present; it also defines the present as the time and space of engaged action – more precisely, of historically engaged actions. Now, as Hans U. Gumbrecht stressed, such a conception of the present is one of the most basic, albeit tacit, premises of historicism. According to Gumbrecht, it is indeed only in the context of historicism that "at each present moment, a person is prone to imagine a range of future situations that must be different from the past and the present, and out of which she chooses a future of his or her liking." In other words, it is only within this context that "subjectivity can integrate the component of action in the self-image that it offers to humanity. And this interrelation of time and action is what creates the impression that humanity can make its own history." Accordingly, it is only within this conceptual/existential context that time, understood as an absolute agent of change, "gives innovation the profile of a compulsory law."[22] As becomes clear "historicity," "historical awareness," "historical purchase," and "historical insight" (and also Marxism and modernism) are stars in the same epistemological constellation – one at whose center lies the historicist worldview. Now, what such evidence unveils is the scale of the challenges that the crisis of historicism poses to so-called progressive criticism: At stake, in the last instance, is the viability not only of a left with no a future (in Clark's words, a left prone to "not to see a shape or logic—a development from past to future," and which therefore leaves behind "in the whole grain and frame of its self-conception, the last afterthoughts and

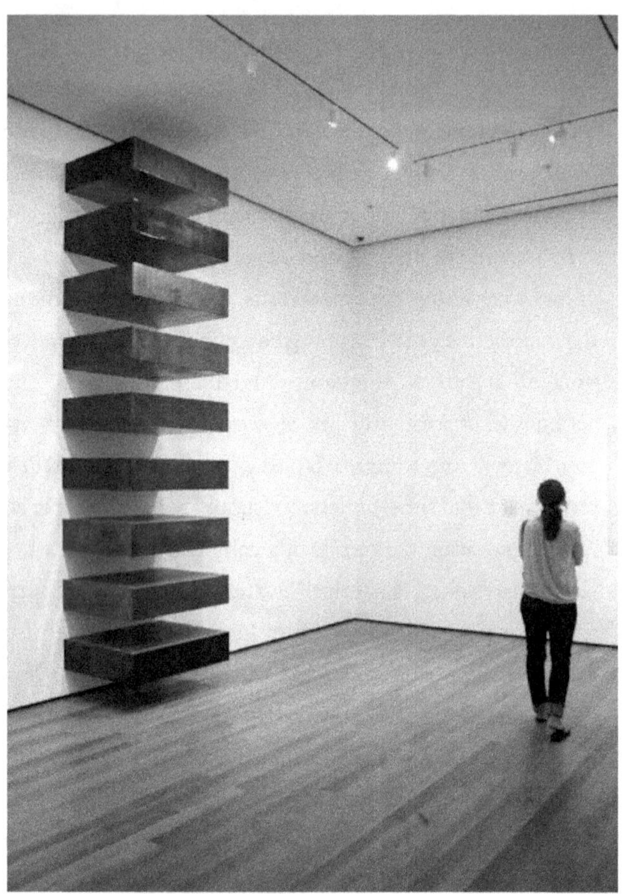

Untitled (Stack), Donald Judd, 1967. MoMA, Nova York NY, 2009.

Foto Otavio Leonidio

images of the avant-garde)[23] but a left that is no longer engaged in "History" – or at least prone to engage in an alternative concept of history. Not by chance, Foster concludes *The Return of the Real* by asking himself whether a dysfunctional postmodern subject (the subject "suspended between obscene proximity and spectacular separation") might simply obey the logic of a "cynical reason [that] does not cancel so much as relinquish agency."[24]

Still, as the reading of *The Return of the Real* makes clear, Foster's allegiance to the modernist/historicist episteme is never at risk. That much is made evident, for example, when he affirms that Michael Fried (knowingly, minimalism's most famous detractor)[25] "is an excellent critic of minimalism, not because he is right in condemn it but because in order to do so persuasively he has to understand it, and this is to understand its threat to late modernism."[26] The claim is preposterous: Fried never understood minimalism, which he regarded solely in terms of its objectness – a reading which is outright reductionist, as Anne M. Wagner noted).[27] What such a claim makes clear, however, is the umbilical affinity between Fried and Foster's critical practices.

It is not surprising, on that account, that notwithstanding his objections to Rosalind Krauss' reading of minimalism[28] (which he sees as excessively phenomenological) Foster is also prone to see minimalism as a typically phenomenological, environmental manifestation – in his words, as an art that prompts the viewer "to explore the perceptual consequences of a particular intervention in a given site. This is the fundamental reorientation that minimalism inaugurates."[29] That such reading (suitable to the post-minimalist work of the second Robert Morris, and also to the phenomenological objects of Richard Serra) implies, for example, an absurd reduction of the meaning of Donald Judd's work is one of the consequences of Foster's ideological bias. That it is totally unfit to the essentially anti-phenomenological, anti-site-specific work of Robert Smithson, is another.

**FROM A PSYCHOANALYTIC PERSPECTIVE,
ONE MAY SAY THAT IN HIS COMMITMENT TO
DE-REPRESS THE REAL, FOSTER ENDED UP
REPRESSING THE MINIMALIST REAL**

– something Joseph Kosuth had pointed out with regard to the historiographical constructions set up by the lineage of critics to which Foster is connected. Indeed, as Kosuth put it, minimalism's "assimilation into the mainstream as another kind of form in the history of sculpture" ensued nothing less than "the cleansing of its philosophical, much less ideological, weight."[30]

None of that diminishes the relevance of *The Return of the Real*. Originally published in 1996, but including key stretches first made public in the mid-1980s, the book lays bare that several of the questions raised by 1960s art still drive, and to a large extent haunt, current art praxis and criticism. Yet the book's relevance does not stem so much from its findings as it does from the way in which it reveals, albeit unwittingly, the challenges and quandaries that the crisis of the modern concept of history poses to contemporary critical (or post-critical) thinking – Hal Foster's included.

NOTES

AN. I appreciate the readings and comments of Marcelo G. Jasmin, Felipe Charbel and Henrique Estrada.

EN. This article is a rreview of the book *The Return of the Real*. Article previously published at: Otavio Leonidio, "O real e a história," *Novos Estudos Cebrap* 101, January/March 2015, 175-182.

1. Hal Foster, *The Return of the Real* (Cambridge: MIT Press, 1996), 10.

2. Robert Smithson, "Ultramodern," *Arts Magazine* 42, September/October 1967, 31.

3. Foster, *The Return*, 5.

4. Ibdi., 29.

5. Peter Bürger, *Theory of the Avant-Garde* (Minneapolis: University of Minnesota Press, 1984).

---

6. Foster, *The Return*, 5.

7. "Repressed by numerous post-structuralisms, the real has returned, only as a traumatic real," page 239, note 38. In its original formulation, that caveat was even stricter: "Repressed by various poststructuralisms, the real has returned – but not just any real, only the traumatic real." Foster, "What's new about the neo-avant-garde?," *October* 70, Autumn 1994, 29.

8. Foster, *The Return*, 217.

9. That is to say, averse to "the false pluralism of the post-historical museum, market and academia." Ibdi., X.

10. Ibdi., 5.

11. Ibdi., X.

12. T.J. Clark, "For a Left with No Future," *New Left Review* 74, March/April 2012, newleftreview.org/II/74/t-j-clark-for-a-left-with-no-future.

13. Foster, *The Return*, 14.

14. Ibdi., XV.

15. Harold Rosenberg, "The New as Value," in Harold Rosenberg, *The Anxious Object* (New York: Horizon Press, 1964), 227.

16. Foster, *The Return*, 5.

17. Slavoj Zizek, quoted in Foster, *The Return*, 240.

18. Foster, *The Return*, 14.

19. See Reinhart Koselleck, *Futures Past: On the Semantics of Historical Time* (Cambridge: MIT Press, 1985).

20. Hannah Arendt, "The concept of history: ancient and modern," in *Between Past and Future: Eight Exercises in Political Thought* (New York: Viking Press, 1961), 63.

21. Foster, *The Return*, XIII.

22. Hans U. Gumbrecht, "Cascatas de Modernidade," in Hans U. Gumbrecht, *Modernização dos Sentidos* (São Paulo: Editora 34, 1998), 15-16.

23. Clark, "Future."

24. Foster, *The Return*, 222-223.

25. Michael Fried, "Art and Objecthood," *Artforum* 10, Summer 1967, 12-23.

26. Foster, *The Return*, 53.

27. Anne M. Wagner, "Reading minimal art," in *Minimal Art: A Critical Anthology, ed. Gregory Battcock* (Berkeley: University of California Press, 1995).

28. See Rosalind Krauss, "Sense and Sensibility: Reflection on Post '60s Sculpture," *Artforum* 3, November 1973, 43-53.

29. Foster, *The Return*, 38.

30. Joseph Kosuth, "History for" [1988], in Joseph Kosuth, *Art after philosophy and after. Collected Writing 1966-1990* (Cambridge: MIT Press, 1991), 240.

Leonidio, Otavio

T2660   Risky Space / Otavio Leonidio; editors: Abilio
Guerra, Fernando Luiz Lara e Silvana Romano Santos. -- São
Paulo : Romano Guerra ; Austin : Nhamerica, 2017.
280 p. : il. (Latin America: Thoughts ; 3)

ISBN: 978-85-88585-65-2 (Romano Guerra)
ISBN: 978-1-946070-04-3 (Nhamerica)

1.History of architecture - Brazil 2.History of urbanism - Brazil
3.Modern architecture 4.Sustainable design 5.Architecture design
I.Lara, Fernando Luiz, ed. II.Santos, Silvana Romano, ed. III.Title
IV.Serie

CDD 724.981

Romano Guerra Editora
Rua General Jardim 645 cj 31
01223-011 São Paulo SP Brasil
rg@romanoguerra.com.br
www.romanoguerra.com.br

Nhamerica Plataform
807 E 44th st,
Austin, TX, 78751 USA
editors@nhamericaplatform.com
www.nhamericaplatform.com

COVER IMAGE
Photo Otavio Leonidio

This book was composed in Alegreya and Raleway
Printed in paper Offset 90g and Duodesign 250g